SAGA TREES

Glenny Fletcher

SAGA TREES

The Sutton-Dudley Family History
from 1066-1899

Glenny Fletcher

BREWIN BOOKS

BREWIN BOOKS
19 Enfield Ind. Estate,
Redditch,
Worcestershire,
B97 6BY
www.brewinbooks.com

First published by Brewin Books 2025

Front cover: Dudley Castle.
Rear cover: Robert Dudley courted Queen Elizabeth at Kenilworth Castle in 1575. English Heritage recreated the knot garden as a complete experience there in 2009. Photo taken by the author at this time.

A CIP catalogue record for this book is available from the British Library.

ISBN: 978-1-85858-788-2

Printed and bound in Great Britain
by Hobbs the Printers Ltd.

Contents

For Clare, a special Jackson, with love.

Acknowledgements

MANY THANKS to the authors and editors of cited sources, information professionals, including librarians, webmasters and content managers online. Thank you so much to every historian who threw light on darkness. Another big thanks goes to the illustrators for their inspired drawings and to Katharine Wiseman for her excellent indexing and 'extra mile' helpfulness. Brewin Books can be recommended for their constructive help and professional services. Special 'thanks' to friends and family for their encouragement from a distance during the lockdowns of 2020-2021.

Introduction

WHILE *SAGA TREES* tracks a family history spanning 1066-1899, the book narrates a chronological slice of Britain's past, a page turner with a twist. Long hidden events through wars and peaceful times emerge. Chapter by chapter, century by century, beginning with the Sutton Dudley lines, the families in question relate to various noble houses. Their deeds eventually herald industrial progress, which unfolds within these covers. Which path will *Saga Trees* take? Discover fascinating glimpses into Georgian and Victorian periods, including unexpected, bordering on uncanny, coincidence and surprise along the way. Many surnames arise within, maybe yours is among them? Lots of footnotes and a detailed index enhance the narrative with the added benefit of *Saga Trees* doubling as a reference book.

Chapter 1

Noble Normans?

THE SAGA begins with ancestors of the Sutton and Dudley families.

William I – reigned 1066-1087

William's conquest of England took remorseless force. His occupying army completely took over the rule of Anglo-Saxon England and attempts at revolt failed. The outcome was that Duke William of Normandy, a foreign king, took over the ownership of England. His mainly Norman followers, plus some French and others, shared the land grab, taking the titles and massive estates offered by William, now King not a mere Duke. They accepted the Conqueror's offers for reasons of personal advancement and greed, which had been their purpose for joining the invasion. However, land gifts could revert to the monarch at any time because barons as vassals held their lands on military tenure.

The Conqueror brought a governing elite of Norman noblemen – except that Dudley and Weoley received a Picard not a Norman, William FitzAnsculf.[1] Taken in this context, Dudley and Weoley barons differed because they came from the area of the River Somme. The Conqueror was thankful for FitzAnsculf, probably admiring his viciousness as a soldier, also FitzAnsculf possessed the qualities of command, noble arts and shrewdness expected of him by his comrades as well as by the Conqueror. Held in such

1 *Picardy History* (FrenchProperty.com IFP Ltd) *https://www.regions-of-france.com/regions/picardy/history#* [accessed 21 March 2020].

high esteem and granted vast territories in the Midlands and elsewhere by William, FitzAnsculf needed a hilltop castle to oversee the security of his Midland terrain from all directions. Dudley Castle Hill (Coneygre) was the chosen spot for Dudley's Motte and Bailey wooden defences.

Early 11th century Dudley had been owned by Anglo-Saxon Earl Edwin whose land was confiscated after the Conquest. Before 1066, some tenants-in-chief had a large number of fiefs, known as an honour or barony, hence the 'honor of Dudley'. Each had its own court, judging tenants' cases. All who owed knights' service attended, mostly to sort out disputes such as who was allowed to use which lots of land. Norman England was identified as much by continuity as change according to modern historians. Previously, patterns in evidence had been misinterpreted and it was thought that William's feudal system was very different from Anglo-Saxon ways.

After 1066 the status of tenants-in-chief was lower than thegns before, they were now on a par with canons and bishops. Prior to the Conquest, great earls were serious challengers to the King, in wealth and power, with thousands of thegns loyal to them and huge revenues from their extensive landholdings. They were then the King's military leaders and swore loyalty

Dudley Medieval Castle, drawing by Eileen Wale.

to him. This mattered when threats of invasion arose but turned out to be less important. Earldoms became smaller as Normans replaced Anglo-Saxons with tenants-in-chief, who each paid homage to the King in return for land – and who would have to forfeit these lands if they failed him – not ideal and there was a revolt of barons in 1075. The economic demands on many peasants may have increased because the Normans wanted to extract more revenue from England than had been the case under Edward the Confessor. All members of society had to meet demands, which caused disgruntlement.

Tenants-in-chief were granted land and other privileges in return for military service offset by tax and reliefs in addition to duties of overseeing justice and manorial courts. Some historians described the extremes of Norman Conquest and Norman England as the colonisation of a military state. Financial significance made a great impact because many of King William's tenants-in-chief enjoyed special deals, such as not having to pay geld tax on some of their lands.

The greatest change was loss of economic control in England and the power of Norman control, most obviously by building castles, rebuilding churches and raising cathedrals in stone. Both Anglo-Saxons and Normans adapted quite quickly, blending into an Anglo-Norman culture. Anglo-Saxon England was much richer and more sophisticated than Normandy, therefore Normans rapidly adopted many English ways. The monarch possibly had a plan to reverse some of the privileges he gave as a way of extracting more money from tenants: heavy geld taxes had to be paid in 1084 and 1086. The *Domesday Book*[2] might have indicated only how many extra soldiers were needed in each Hundred of land by tenants-in-chief should an invasion come. In his last year, 1087, the Conqueror was confident of having absolute rule and demanded an oath to be sworn from each of his followers. The way *Domesday* was organised, with the holdings of each tenant-in-chief itemised by shire, resulted in an excellent guide for understanding how financial opportunities arose whenever a tenant-in-chief died or forfeited a fief. *Domesday* included many claims for Anglo-Saxon lands to be returned and it showed Dudley to be in the Hundred of Clent, Worcestershire.

The Lord and 'tenant-in-chief' in 1086 was William, son of Ansculf, whereas in 1066 Earl Edwin had been lord. There were two leagues of

2 *Domesday Book* (1086).

woodland, one smith, three villagers, ten smallholders and two slaves. The value to the lord in 1086 was £3, down £1 from 1066.[3] Nearby Tettenhall had two entries in *Domesday*, showing William as lord in 1086. Tettenhall 2 was lorded by Tettenhall canons, by 1086 these men were recorded as canons of Wolverhampton (St. Mary).[4] Medieval life was structured within the three institutions of manor, church and vill: Coventry and Lichfield shared the Diocese that served Dudley. Feudal Dudley Castle Hill ground was of the shire of Worcester whereas its surroundings were of the shire of Stafford. Sedgley 1 in the Hundred of Seisdon, Staffordshire, was much more valuable to its lord and tenant-in-chief William, son of Ansculf, being £10 in 1086.[5] Also, Sedgley was a major and valuable royal vill (township) in 1086 when held by King William. The township of Cotwallend was in woodland that was historically located in the royal forest of Kinver. Sandwall Field was for communal use throughout its parish.[6]

William I's introduction of forestry control had reinforced his authority over the land but adversely affected relationships with his subjects. Peasants were denied access to the best meat, which reduced their diet for over a century. Five Ways, Birmingham, and Edgbaston Church were forested and on an historic road route although it was disadvantageous to be in the valley of the River Rea. This was just one of many parts of the Midlands also received by William Ansculf from William I. By Edward II's reign (1307-1327) the Lord of that manor was Henry de Edgbaldeston.[7] Dargue relates the perspective of Wulfwin, Richard's Anglo-Saxon predecessor, [who] held [this land] freely in the time of King Edward:[8]

---

3 *Open Domesday, The first free online copy of Domesday Book*, 'Place: Dudley', J.J.N. Palmer, University of Hull. *http://www.domesdaybook.co.uk* [accessed 22 July 2017].

4 *Open Domesday,* 'Place: Tettenhall', [accessed 22 July 2017].

5 *Open Domesday*, 'Place: Sedgley', [accessed 22 July 2017].

6 Dudley Metropolitan Borough Council, 'Township of Sedgley 1750', produced by John Hemingway and Jennifer Foster (Dudley, 2006), bibliog. col. map, pdf 57.24kb. *https://www.dudley.gov.uk/residents/planning/historic-environment/historic-maps-of-dudley/* [accessed 16 October 2020]. (Dudley's historic maps can be viewed from 1307 to the present day). 'Cotwallend Township'.

7 Philip B. Chatwin, *A History of Edgbaston* (Birmingham, 1914). Reprinted from *The Birmingham Archaeological Society's Transactions* (1913).

8 William Dargue, *A History of BIRMINGHAM Places & Place Names from A to Y, A Brief History of Birmingham, Medieval Birmingham 1066-c1530. https://billdargue-jimdargue.com/glossary-brief-histories/a-brief-history-of-birmingham/medieval-birmingham/* [accessed 5 January 2019].

> *From William FitzAnsculf of Dudley Castle, Richard* (presumably Richard de Birmingham) *holds 4 hides in Birmingham. Land for 6 ploughteams. In the demesne* [the lord's own land]: *1 hide, 5 villeins, & 4 bordars, with 2 ploughteams. Woodland half a league long & 2 furlongs* [wide]. *The value was and is 20 shillings.*

Sutton [-on-Trent] was in the Hundred of Lythe, Nottinghamshire, where the Lord in 1086 was Hervey [de Sutton] while the Tenant-in-Chief was Count Alan (of Brittany).[9] The value to the lord in 1086 was £4. De Suttons' lines arose all over the British Isles. Turning specifically to the Nottingham branch, they had a coat of arms showing a wolf's head, which they took to America centuries later. The source of these arms was Hugh (known as Lupus, c.1047-1101) Earl of Chester, born in Normandy, an extremely powerful man. The main home of the de Suttons was Malpas in the Marches on the Cheshire/Flintshire border. Its name means 'bad pass' or 'Depenbach' in Welsh. The ancient castle was Hugh's, while the manor passed through many families, including from the de Suttons to the St. Pierres and others through to the Drakes.[10]

Hugh's father Richard le Goz, Viscount of Avranches, had helped William's conquest by providing 60 ships for the Norman invasion. Richard owned large estates throughout west Normandy, lying to the east of Mont-Saint-Michel which was once part of Brittany. William I saw Hugh's role as a councillor of England and was more than generous to him, trusting him with the command of Tutbury Castle in Staffordshire and making him Chester's 2nd created Norman Earl. Hugh's term ran for 30 years from 1071-1101. Chester Cathedral gained palatine powers because of Cheshire's strategic location in the Welsh Marches.[11 12 13]

The Conqueror turned the Anglo-Welsh border 'the Marsh', into private principalities under the control of his "most important nobles". William

---

9 *Open Domesday*, 'Place: Sutton on Trent', [1 of 3 entries, a very large population]. [Accessed 22 July 2017].

10 UK Genealogy Archives, *Malpas, Cheshire – genealogy heraldry and history – ukga.org*. Transcribed from the *Comprehensive Gazetteer of England & Wales* (1894-1895). *https://ukga.org/index.php?pageid=1160* [accessed 2 June 2020].

11 'Hugh d'Avranches', *The Peerage*. *http://thepeerage.com/p21588.htm* [accessed 13 June 2020].

12 Barry W. Cunliffe, *The Penguin Atlas of British & Irish history* (2001), p.72. *https://books.google.com/books?id=o4IZAQQAAIAAJ* [accessed 20 June 2020].

13 *The New Encyclopaedia Britannica: Micropaedia,* Encyclopaedia Britannica (1995), p.180.

Fitz Osbern, Roger Montgomery and Hugh d'Avranches became the Earls of Hereford, Shrewsbury and Chester respectively. Montgomery as a place was situated nearest to England.[14] The Marches Lords were feudal subjects to the King but they were not part of William I's kingdom. The amount of freedom he allowed them resulted in excessive Norman rule and there were many campaigns against Welsh resistance. Eventually in time, Griffith ap Gwenwynwyn would drop his Prince of Powys title to receive the barony of Powys Castle under the title de la Pole. Powys lay south east from Gwynedd.

Historian Christopher Dyer's interpretation of early medieval urbanism, systematically researched within context, showed the existence of lively and active communities.[15] Dyer was sceptical about the *Domesday Book*; he found Staffordshire's rural population to have been undercounted, reducing the percentage of town dwellers. Actually, country people were omitted over the whole of England. In studying urbanisation, Dyer observed the perspective of tenants not their lords. Some parts of society and the economy showed more continuity than change. Settlement life would have continued much as it had before for most peasants because their lives were dominated by the different demands of the agricultural year and they had disease, bad harvests and personal hardships to face.

The *Domesday Book* had been a tool used by the Conqueror to gain central control. Summaries of landholding surveys allowed his government to see what feudal obligations were owed by his tenants-in-chief. King William had centralised power so that no-one responsible for English government had enough wealth or power to challenge his rule, Dudley lords included. In William son of Ansculf's case £10 was due in 1086.[16] Sedgley was then a most important and valuable royal vill (township), held by the King himself. A priest was recorded in the *Domesday Book* therefore a church probably stood on the site of today's All Saints, Sedgley. The King's local representative probably lived nearby because the landowner normally resided in the grounds of a hall. No coincidence that the Court House (site of the manor's court of jurisdiction) is in the same plot as the church.[17]

---

14 *Kings and Queens*, pp.16-19.

15 'The Urbanization of Staffordshire: The First Phases (1)', Christopher Dyer, lecture given at the 21st Earl Lecture, University of Keele, 9 November 2001, *Staffordshire Studies*, 14 (2002).

16 *Open Domesday*, 'Place: Sedgley', [accessed 22 July 2017].

17 Dudley Metropolitan Borough Council, 'Sedgley Township'.

Two celebrities had similar ancestries to this one, making them distant cousins many times removed: Courteney Cox on the USA television version of *Who Do You Think You Are* and Danny Dyer on the British equivalent.[18] Their reactions differed when they found out. Most of us would find similar relations if we could research 268, 435, 456, great x 26 great-grandparents.[19] Some individuals would be duplicated because that estimate was the population of the whole world in 1066.

Danny Dyer was shocked when he heard he was descended from William the Conqueror, whereas Courteney Cox received the information in an amused yet understated way, comparing her family's story to a real *Game of Thrones*. *The Guardian's* reviewer thought Danny's programme was the greatest *Who Do You Think You Are?* of all because his responses were so hilarious; there are many YouTube clips of Danny's meetings with specialist historians.[20] William I had already been victorious in battles on the continent before 1066 and Danny heard how aggressive the Conqueror was and seemed impressed by "Will's" White Tower in London.

The Vikings had needed to raid and seek food abroad as it was insufficient in their cold homeland. They explored rivers and found Paris. A legendary King of the Vikings, Rollo, attacked the city and did a deal, becoming the first Duke of Normandy, Danny's 31st x great-grandfather. When it came to experiencing Viking food, Danny was a good sport, tasting bits of a sheep's head and consuming off-putting liquid. Thus Danny Dyer discovered that Norsemen were Normans. The story may have been exaggerated by Dudo of Saint-Quentin in his *History of the Normans* circa 986.[21] Rollo of Normandy (c.860-c.930) was a Viking chieftain who became the founder and first ruler of the region of Normandy. He converted to Christianity as part of 'the deal' with King Charles the Simple and was William the Conqueror's 3 x great-grandfather. The *Domesday Book* was undertaken on William's orders one year

---

18 'Who Do You Think You Are? Danny Dyer', BBC [online] (Series 13, 15 November 2016). *https://www.bbc.co.uk/programmes/p04gfg0l* [accessed 3 August 2020].

19 'Who Do You Think You Are? *The Guardian*, USA review – the one where Monica goes in search of her ancestors', *The Guardian* (20 March 2018). *https://www.theguardian.com/tv-and-radio/2018/mar/20/who-do-you-think-you-are-usa-review-monica-courteney-cox-ancestors* [accessed 16 April 2020].

20 'Danny Dyer', YouTube videos. *https://ww.YouTube.com* [accessed 31 July 2020].

21 Joshua J. Mark, *Ancient History Encyclopaedia*, 'Twelve Great Viking Leaders, Rollo of Normandy' (18 December 2018). *https://www.ancient.en/Rollo_of_Normandy/* [accessed 1 August 2020].

before his death.[22] Barons were kept down as much by the strong monarchs that followed William I as they had been by the Conqueror himself.

William II (Rufus) – reigned 1087-1135

John Hunt investigated land use in Dudley 1066-1322, throughout William II's reign and beyond. Here is an abstract from 'Lordship and the Landscape': [23]

> "Examination of both documentary and archaeological evidence made it possible to follow a developing West Midland landscape between the 11th and 14th centuries. In this study, 'landscape' is understood to include land use, settlement and the built environment. It considers the extent to which the honor provided the framework for the activities and relationships of the aristocracy who lived within it, and the extent to which there was a relationship between regional power, that is lordship, and the landscape. Lordship generally worked as an influential factor rather than as a determinant factor. A more direct contribution to settlement patterns and rural landscape came where moated sites, or a monastic house, were established. However castles, monastic foundations, chases and parkland were well beyond the remit of most lords, and only lords of baronial status readily encompassed all of these."

The ancestors of this saga were blessed with vast estates and remits, they seem to have been worthy carers for their territory even if they were more influential than powerful. William Rufus on the other hand was power mad. A second wave of Marcher settlement followed under his orders. Despite their ferocity, the Normans failed to conquer northern Marchia Walliae (the March) and Pura Wallia (deep Wales).[24] There was a core of Welsh revolt in Gwynedd in North Wales in 1094. Hugh d'Avranches was loyal to Rufus and at the court of Henry I he served as a principal councillor. Hugh ruled most of North Wales and was present in 1094. Anglesey was lost and much

---

22 *Kings and Queens of the British Isles*, ed. Thomas Cussans, *The Times* (London, 2015), pp.44-45, illus., maps.

23 'Lordship and the Landscape: a documentary and archaeological study of the Honor of Dudley, c. 1066-1322', by John Hunt in *Brit. Archaeological Reports*, (British Series), CCLXIV, (1997), pp.120-9. *History of Art Bibliography* in *Open Access* (J. and E. Hedges, Oxford, 1997).

24 *Kings and Queens*, pp.16-19.

of Gwynedd. He put up a ferociously savage fight to suppress Welsh revolt, hence his reputation as 'the Wolf'.

Dugdale's *Monasticon Anglicanum* showed an engraving of Hugh Lupus, Earle of Chester:

> "sitting in his parliament with the barons and abbots of that Countie Palatine."[25]

Another name that Hugh brought upon himself was 'the Fat', because he was very overweight later in life although he looked slim in the engraving and presumably would have needed agility as a successful soldier. He gave land endowments to Whitby Abbey in North Yorkshire and founded St. Werburgh's Abbey, Chester, which is where he was first buried after his death on 27 July 1101. Hugh had married Ermentrude of Claremont but his inheritance went to his nephew, Ranulph le Meschin, Earl of Chester, who had Hugh's remains reburied in the Chapter House of Chester Abbey.[26]

Medieval artefacts discovered at Weoley Castle (Birmingham) included fragments of blue Syrian glass depicting the image of a swan, described as indicative of the family's status.[27] Crusaders, including from Weoley, attempted to recover the Holy Land from Islam rule between at least 1096 and 1271; continuity outran change before and after the Crusades. The Knights Templar headquarters was the fortress of Tortosa in Syria.

Henry I – reigned 1100-1135

Henry I was good at controlling his competitive and ambitious barons. He was the only son of the Conqueror to have been born in England. Unlike his siblings, he was literate, hence his nickname 'beauclerc' meaning 'good writer'. In an English throne steal, he outmanoeuvred Robert, Duke of Normandy, freshly back from the Holy Land. Being holy did not seem to curb Norman aggression but Henry used his diplomatic skills to get the better of Robert.[28]

---

25 William Dugdale, *Monasticon Angicanum* (edition of 1718), illus. of engraving of Earle of Chester, Hugh Lupus.

26 C.P. Lewis, 'Avranches, Hugh, d'. First Earl of Chester (d. 1101)' in *Oxford Dictionary of National Biography* online edn., *https://www.oxforddnb.com* (unseen).

27 Birmingham Museums & Art Gallery, *Weoley Castle Birmingham* (2011), illus.

28 *Kings and Queens*, pp.44-45, 54-57.

Stephen – reigned 1135-1154

When Stephen, nephew of Henry I, came to the throne in 1135 stability ebbed away. Matilda, Henry's daughter was disliked and faced discrimination. By 1140, the then Earl of Chester allied himself to Matilda and her half-brother in an 1140 rebellion. Five years later, the Normans won when Matilda was defeated by Stephen at the Battle of Faringdon. It was her son Henry II who overthrew Stephen to become the first Angevin monarch of England. Norman family feuds exceeded greed concerning the English crown, however they desired the dukedom of Normandy more as it was the most powerful dukedom in France, England to them was a mere colony. French royal policy was to weaken Normandy, which involved England in power struggles.

Chapter 2

Able Angevins?

ANGEVIN KINGS of England between 1154 and 1399 are so called because they were originally Counts of Anjou in France. They were part of the Plantagenets' dynasty, which ruled in England for 331 years. Until Richard II was deposed in 1399, the Kings were more French than English.[29]

Henry II – reigned 1154-1189

Matilda's son, Duke Henry Plantagenet succeeded Henry I in 1154, he tried to conquer Wales in 1165; marked by the Treaty of Woodstock. His grand-daughter, Ida Longspee, married Ralph de Somery, 7th Dudley Baron, whose barony term was 1210-1216. Variations in spelling were normal, people went by the sounds of words such as Longspee or Longespee, the Paganels (alt. de Paganels with one or two 'lls') came from France and Brittany. Dudley Priory was founded in 1160 by Gervase Paganel as a dependency of Much Wenlock and was dedicated to St. James' Cluniac order.[30] Chitham found no record that Fulke Paganel married a FitzAnsculf daughter although it was evident that Fulke held all FitzAnsculf's former possessions, including Newport Pagnall, Buckinghamshire – another variation of the Paganell surname's spelling and the foundation of another Cluniac order.[31]

---

29 *Kings and Queens of the British Isles*, ed. Thomas Cussans, *The Times* (London, 2015), pp.68-69, illus., maps.

30 M.W. Greenslade and D.G. Stuart, *A History of Staffordshire*, 3rd edn., (Chichester, 1998), pp. 33, 81, map. (Darwen History Series).

31 Edward Chitham, *The Story of Dudley* (Stroud, 2014), illus.

There are difficulties with the chronology of the de Somery Dudley barons. British History Online (BHO) is a trustworthy source, as is Cracroft's.[32] Hart et al compiled a family history in 1972 which was later uploaded online at *Our Folk*, electronically combining genealogies to create a consensus of opinion, which tends to compare very well with many of the online de Somery family trees.[33] [34] Discrepancies in individual trees appeared to be ironed out – the resulting content must have been thoroughly researched prior to inputting into an early computer. *Our Folk* traces the name de Somery back to Saxon times. Ralph de Somery was born in 1100, the origin of the surname probably came from Sommery in the valley of the River Somme, Picardy.

Richard I (Lionheart) – reigned 1189-1199

England was useful for Richard I to finance foreign ventures, he was remembered for the Third Crusade he led jointly with Philippe II of France, which aimed to liberate Jerusalem. They disagreed en route to the Holy Land. Although Cyprus was captured, the success of their further mission was debatable.

John – reigned 1199-1216

The de Greys, had been living at Greys Court, Oxfordshire, since the *Domesday Book*. By the mid-13th century the estate belonged to Walter de Grey (d. 1255). He was a powerful and wealthy magnate who was also a reforming Archbishop of York. De Grey supported King John by agreeing to the *Magna Carta* in 1215 and he was named in the charter. Subsequently he was Regent of England during Henry III's absence abroad.[35] Sir John de Grey (1271-1312) was a professional soldier who was probably responsible for fortifying Greys Court with substantial masonry curtain walls and towers.[36] This family research tells a story similar to John Bird's, who was the subject of an article in

---

32 *Cracroft's Peerage: The Complete Guide to the British Peerage & Baronetage.*

33 BHO, 'Parishes: Dudley' in *A History of the County of Worcester,* Vol. 3 (London: orig. pub. by Victoria County History, 1913), pp.90-105. *http://www.british-history.ac.uk/vch/worcs/vol3* [accessed 21 November 2016].

34 *Our Folk Free Online Family Tree,* de Somery family (last updated 2002). *http://www.coltechpub.com/hartgen/htm/de-somery.htm* [accessed 7 July 2016]. Based on *Our Folk*, compiled by Albert Thomas Hart, et al. (1972).

35 *Magna Carta* (1216).

36 *A souvenir guide, Greys Court, Oxfordshire* (National Trust, available 2019), illus.

The Bugle.[37] John traces his line back to the barons of Dudley Castle, as does this saga except that John's line may not have linked in at the same point along the de Sutton line. He found direct ancestors among de Somerys and Paganels, stating that Hawise de Somery was brother to his 25th great-grandmother Gervase whose husband had the St. James Priory built. It is interesting that John also reportedly describes the wife of Ralph de Somery as his 24th great-grandmother Margaret Marshal (alt. Marshall), the sister of the Earl of Pembroke. When Ralph died in 1210, Margaret married Maurice de Gant.

The de Somerys had many lands to control and owed many services to the crown. Around 1216, John de Somery received the manor of Bury from Hugh de Semere as fourth part of a fee. Previously Ralph Carbonel held the assize of bread and beer of all his tenants in that manor. It continued within de Somery hands until 1401 when it was alienated by John de Somery to John de Boune.[38] William Percival de Somery, brother of Ralph II, was born the year Henry III came to the throne.

Henry III – reigned 1216-1272

Back in 1086, William I had ignored the lease of Great Gaddesden Manor in the county of Hertford and granted it to the Earl of Salisbury. It passed down to Isabella (or Ela), who married William Longespee, an illegitimate son of Henry II. By right of his wife's title, Longespee became Earl of Salisbury. As his widow, Isabella founded Lacock Abbey in 1232 and became a nun there, later an abbess. Her great-granddaughter Margaret inherited the title, her husband was Henry de Lacy, Earl of Lincoln.[39]

In 1247, Henry III accepted the Treaty of Montgomery. Powis Castle was built circa 1252 and, in the Middle Ages, Powis land covered two thirds of the modern county and extended into the West Midlands.[40]

---

37 'John's ancestral quest results in history book' in *The Bugle* (27 March 2019), p.11. John Bird, *My Journey Back in Time*. Reportedly available by emailing newworld@mymail.com

38 Francis Blomefield, 'Hundred of Diss: Dickleburgh' in *An Essay Towards a Topographical History of the County of Norfolk: Vol.1* (Originally pub. by W. Miller London, 1805), pp.191-205. British History Online [accessed 7 September 2016]. Fn. 33 The family of the Semeres, or So. Merys are very ancient: besides those mentioned as lords. I find Jordan de Semere lived in Ed. the First's time.

39 BHO, 'Parishes: Great Gaddesden' in *A History of the County of Hertford,* Vol. 2, ed. William Page (London, 1908). *https://www.british-history.ac.uk/vch/herts/vol2/pp201-207* [accessed 25 June 2020].

40 Mick Powis, *Powis Pages: The People of the Rural Area. A History of the Powis Family,* trudy.weaver@myself.com, All Rights Reserved. 4trudy.co.uk/history.php [accessed 19 June 2020].

The Bugle article about John Bird mentions that Roger de Somery was married to Nicola de Albini. Amabel Chacombe (circa 1235-1281) became Roger's second wife after Nicola died in Dudley Castle circa 1240. Both family histories find Roger de Somery (1238-1272) married to Nichola d'Albini.[41] Notice the variation of spelling, which is quite usual at a time when Anglo-Saxon speech was slowly blending with incoming French language. Nobles spoke French; Latin was the language of the Catholic religion. The gradual change of language would have brought adaptation of communication over a lengthy period of time.

Major Peerages tell us that a second Barons' War 1264-1266 was led by Simon de Montford, who died in that battle. When peace came, Roger II de Somery helped to update the *Magna Carta* as he was one of seven lords chosen to help prelates formulate the *Dictum of Kenilworth.*[42]

Around 1272, Roger granted the right to hold a market and eight-day fair in Newport Paganell.[43] This means that both the Paganells and the De Somerys were active in the town, which becomes relevant to this saga in James I's reign.

Forestation reached its height around 1200 much of Staffordshire's wooded area was used for carts, ploughs, implements, as well as cups, bowls and other treenware. Wood was also burnt into charcoal and wood ashes while ropes were twisted from lime bark (bast). Lords still enjoyed a high quality of living, for example eating sheep and deer which was denied to the peasantry. Following a fire, Roger de Somery of Dudley Castle rebuilt Weoley in 1264 during Henry III's reign.

Edward I – reigned 1272-1307

Edward I was a brutal conqueror of Wales, 1277. The independent existence of Wales finally ended under the *Statute of Wales 1284* when Edward gave his son the permanent title of Prince of Wales in 1301.[44] Griffith ap Gwenwynwyn dropped his Prince of Powys title to receive the barony of Powys Castle under the title de la Pole.

Lay landlords had been disappointed in the profits obtainable from their more remote and infertile estates. Some founded boroughs and markets in

41 John Hemingway, *An Illustrated Chronicle of the Castle and Barony of Dudley 1070-1057* (Dudley, 2006), pp.20-21, 30-31, 48-49. All Rights Reserved.

42 *Dictum of Kenilworth* formulated to improve *Magna Carta* after the Barons' War 1264-1266.

43 Patent Rolls, R of D, Vol. 11, p.45.

44 Parliament, *Statute of Wales* (1284).

a bid to raise revenue from non-agricultural sources. The Somery family as lords of Dudley Castle held some rather bleak and thinly populated manors in the vicinity and so Dudley had raised an extra £8 per annum to incomes from rents and tolls, according to the Hundred Rolls survey commissioned by Edward I in 1273.[45] [46]

Value was added when peasants and rural artisans traded in urban markets where more produce could be sold. Many rural dwellers of the West Midlands found employment in industrial pursuits. Dudley's lords seem to have been unafraid of developing and pursuing new ideas, there would have been risks to consider but they took them. Dugdale is a rich source of Dudley medieval history, as is Cracroft's Peerage and Burke's Peerage.[47] [48] [49] [50]

Edward I commissioned a great inquiry into landholding in England in 1279 that went far beyond, and indeed was far superior, to that found in the *Domesday Book* of 1086.[51] *Domesday* mentioned the number of villeins and cottars in each manor but omitted their names, their obligations and the size of their holding.[52] The 1279 survey gave all three, both for unfree peasants – villeins and serfs – and for numerous freeholders, who had either been ignored or had not existed at the time of the *Domesday* survey. Edward and his advisers seem to have had a general idea of a grander *Domesday* to which everyone could appeal for proof of their rights. There were two problems:

45 'Small Towns in the East and West Midlands in the Later Middle Ages: A Comparison' by Jane Laughton and Christopher Dyer in *Midland History*, 24(1), pp.24-52 (1999, online 18 July 2013), p.36, *http://dx.doi.org/10.1179/mdh.1999.24.1.24* [accessed 30 May 2017]. Fn. 44 'Lordship and the Landscape: a Documentary and Archaeological Study of the Honor of Dudley, c. 1066-1322', by John Hunt in *Brit. Archaeological Reports* (British Series) CCLXIV, pp.120-129, (1997).

46 *Hundredorum Rolls* (1273). *https://www.houseofnames.com/blogs/Hundred-Rolls* [accessed 20 July 2020].

47 William Dugdale, *Dugdale's Antiquities of Warwickshire*, 2nd edn. Hundreds drawn by Henry Beighton (1730), 2 vols., illus. by Wenceslaus Hollar, (1st ed. 1656).

48 *Cracroft's Peerage: The Complete Guide to the British Peerage & Baronetage.*

49 Bernard Burke, Knight, *Burke's Genealogical and Heraldic History of the Landed Gentry* (London, 1939).

50 William Dugdale, *Baronage of England* (1675).

51 *Domesday Book* (1086).

52 David Carpenter, Review of *A Second Domesday? The Hundred Rolls of 1279-80, Reviews in History* (review no. 691). *http://www.history-ac.uk/reviews/review/691* [accessed 14 June 2019]. Sandra Raban, *A Second Domesday? The Hundred Rolls of 1279-80* (Oxford, 2004). P. Hyams, *Kings, Lords and Peasants: The Common Law of Villeinage in the Twelfth and Thirteenth Centuries* (Oxford, 1980).

the first concerned procedure, namely deciding just how litigants could call upon *The Hundred Rolls*, the second was more contentious when deciding who exactly could appeal and in what circumstances.[53] The King envisioned an entirely royal authority. Given the problems of deciding how exactly *The Hundred Rolls* could meet their stated purpose, no decisions were ever made. This outcome would have affected manorial lords.

Coal and iron mines were known to have been worked in Dudley as early as 1291.[54] This perspective needs to be remembered in the context of unusual compared with usual medieval activity. Some would say 'lucky' and 'plucky' Roger de Somery had a mine of 'sea coal' worth 13s 4d; yearly, a mine of iron and sea coal worth 40s, and two great smithies of the annual value of £4.[55] This could be seen as simply being fortunate or being capable of making one's own fortune in an area that was so rich in minerals.

Christopher Dyer judged the sophistication of an urban system by assessing its network and hierarchy. Staffordshire's network achieved a virtually complete coverage to the extent that by the late 1200s almost everyone in the countryside lived within six miles of a town, particularly in adjacent counties, examples were Dudley (in Worcestershire), Newport and Market Drayton in Shropshire and Ashbourne in Derbyshire. South-east towns such as Dudley and Halesown (later joined by Stourbridge) crowded each other.[56] Dudley's lords seem to have kept and controlled their surroundings well.

Examples of original sources[57] [58] in translation from Latin are:

> "the charter of John de Somery to Richard Russell concerning the site for a stall".

---

53 *The Hundred Rolls* (1279-80).

54 'Small Towns in the East and West Midlands in the Later Middle Ages' p.44. Fn. 80 J.R. Birrell, 'Peasant craftsmen in the medieval forest' in *Agric. Hist. Rev*, XVII (1969) [and more sources].

55 BHO, 'Parishes: Dudley'. Fn. 161 Worc. Inq. p.m. (Worcs. Hist. Soc.), pt i, pp.76, 107.

56 'The Urbanization of Staffordshire: The First Phases (1)', Christopher Dyer, lecture given at the 21st Earl Lecture, University of Keele, 9 November 2001, *Staffordshire Studies*, 14 (2002).

57 'A Charter to Richard Russell, of Land in Dudley on which he might erect a Stall', *John de Somery, baron of Dudley*, in *Dudley: the medieval town*, translated by John Roper (1968).

58 Ancient deeds preserved, p.10. Source not known. Fn. 2 Dudley Archives? (48/24) (a). Grant undated by William son of Guy, with the consent of Richard his son to William the Cook. Large seal of green wax, almost perfect. Thereon a pear-shaped shield charged with two lions passant (for Somery). Legend: (Maltese type cross) SIGILLVM RAD [VLFI} DE SYMERI.

> "the grant of Ralph de Somery to William Cook of Wombourne for an assart for the rent of 12d. On the payment of two marks, which had a large seal of green wax. Thereon a pear-shaped shield charged with two lions passant (for Somery). Legend: [Maltese type cross] SIGILLVM RAD [VLFI] DE SYMERI."

Dudley Priory added Wombourne to an endowment in medieval times. Confirmation of ownership came from the Pope in a document noting Wombourne's status. The Priory's possessions in Sedgley, Wombourne and Northfield were subject to tithes.[59]

Power expressed through owning forest land put the King above all outsiders, indeed the term 'forest' came from the Latin for 'outside'. Hunting was important to the Dudley and de Sutton barons. The royal forest unfairly fed nobility while those of lower status went hungry and animals were protected. Inevitably resentment grew on this and other issues. In 1291 a grant of thirty live bucks from the parks of Sedgley and Dudley was made by King Edward I to Bogo de Knovill. Also, it is known from 1291 that one of the traditional services villagers must do in Sedgley was cutting rushes; this task was worth £1 6s 7d, a profitable amount payable to the manorial lord.[60]

Himley was a vill described in the 1300 perambulation of Kinver as partly or wholly afforested after 1154 and that a Richard de Sutton had free warren granted at Ekering.[61] In feudal times, Himley Hall, near Dudley Castle, had been a manor house, with a moat, beside a medieval church and village. The Dudleys developed Himley Hall as an alternative home from Dudley Castle. Constance carried the Dudley 19th barony title until she died in 1432.

---

59 BHO, 'Parishes: Dudley', Fn. 182 Cal. Close, 1288-1296, p.182. (correct).

60 Dudley Metropolitan Borough Council, 'Township of Sedgley 1750', produced by John Hemingway and Jennifer Foster (Dudley, 2006), bibliog. col. map, pdfs. *https://www.dudley.gov.uk/residents/planning/historic-environment/historic-maps-of-dudley/* [accessed 16 October 2020]. (Dudley's historic maps can be viewed from 1307 to the present day). 'Sedgley Township'.

61 Robert Thoroton, 'Eykering' in *Thoroton's History of Nottinghamshire*: vol. 3, republished with large additions by John Throsby, ed. John Throsby (Nottingham, 1796) pp.195-199. *https://www.british-history.ac.uk/thoroton-notts/vol3/pp195-199* [accessed 25 June 2020]. Fn.14 Esc. 2. E. 1. n. 17. Robert de Sutton, son of William left his son Richard eight years old... Fn. 15 Ch. 34 E. 1: m. 20 free warren granted at Eykering.

Edward I was Courteney Cox's great x 26 grandparent.[62] Sadie's saga headed up the same line at a later date when John VI de Sutton (b.1422) married Elizabeth Berkeley.

Edward II – reigned 1307-1327

The advowson of the Priory of Dudley only seems to have belonged to founder Gervase Paganel and his descendants. By 1323 it was assigned to Margaret, wife of John I de Sutton, Dudley 14th baron, as part of her share of the lands of her brother John de Somery.[63] Enfeoffed had passed his estates to John de Somery in 1319, John Sutton Dudley's 14th barony term was 1322-1325 but he was not a direct ancestor within this saga.

Powis Archives contain material dating back to the 1300s; documentation of Powis ancestry goes back to a Roman Emperor but could be inaccurate. Lords Powis were descendants of the Cherleton (alt. Charlton) and Herbert families, their surnames were not Powis. There had been at the most only 100,000 population in Wales in the Middle Ages, genealogies were very accurate. It is a fact that anyone visiting Ironbridge World Heritage Centre can be certain that people with the surname Powis,

> "dug the coal, to smelt the iron that built the Ironbridge." [64]

Online family history websites reveal that Robert de Cherleton was father of John 1st Lord Cherleton of Powis, whose wife was Hawise Gadarn (born de la Pole), they married in 1309 and are direct ancestors. Hawise was known as 'The Lady of Powis' as well as 'The Hardy of Cherleton'. Their son John Cherleton 1st, was Governor of Builth Castle and was recorded as King's Yeoman on 18 September 1307, the year of the succession of Edward II. Also, it is known that he was Chamberlain in the Royal Household when Prince Edward became King. His children included John, Baron Cherleton 2nd and Isabella, wife of John II, Sutton 1st, Dudley Baron 16th. These two

---

62 'Who Do You Think You Are? *The Guardian*, USA review – the one where Monica goes in search of her ancestors', *The Guardian* (20 March 2018). *https://www.theguardian.com/tv-and-radio/2018/mar/20/who-do-you-think-you-are-usa-review-monica-courteney-cox-ancestors* [accessed 16 April 2020].

63 BHO, 'Parishes: Dudley'. Fn.194 *Cal. Close*, 1318-1323, p.630.

64 Mick Powis, *Powis Pages: The People of the Rural Area. A History of the Powis Family*, trudy.weaver@myself.com. All Rights Reserved.

Johns are often confused by genealogists. John Cherleton 2nd would become Speaker of the Commons and Treasurer of Henry IV's Household.

Also in the Cherleton family, two grand daughters each took a moiety concerning Great Gaddesden Manor. Both were married, Maud to Robert Holand at that time, Ellen to her second husband Alan de Cherleton. A partition of Great Gaddesden Manor was made in 1325, which suited Robert because he had been complicit in the Earl of Lancaster's insurrection and was beheaded in 1328. His own land had been forfeited then but not Ellen's. The Holand(e) family experienced many similar events well into the 1400s and those involved included John Lord Grey de Ruthyn.[65]

Sir Hugh le Despenser the Elder was the first and last Earl of Winchester. It is often overlooked that London, as the capital of England, only served Roman Britannia until 410 AD. The capital of Wessex was Winchester until 927 AD but this gradually changed as London on Thames slowly replaced Winchester, although London did not formally become the British national capital again until 1707-1801.

Hugh and his son the Younger, of the same name, were unpopular favourites of Edward II, homosexuality was rumoured. The Elder was the King's chief advisor and had fought for Edward I in France and Scotland. The Younger was summoned to Parliament as a baron in 1295 and appointed King's Chamberlain in 1318. His wife was Lady Eleanor (b. de Clare 1292-1377), and she was grand daughter to King Edward I. The magnates despised the Despenser's wealth and thought the Younger arrogant. Gilbert de Clare (1243-1295) was Sadie's saga 25th generation ancestor.

Hatred spilled over into an attack in 1321 on both Hughes. At the rebellion of Roger Mortimer with Isabella of France (the 'She Wolf' wife of Edward II) and after a trial in name on 26 October 1326, the Elder was hanged the next day (unless this hanging was staged as some historians believe). Isabella certainly deeply resented the Despensers' relationships with her husband. The story goes that the Elder was hung in his armour then beheaded; his head then displayed in Winchester, his burial place Tewkesbury Abbey. A month later, Edward II was captured in Wales and taken, with Hugh the Younger, to Kenilworth Castle. The Younger was executed at Hereford.

65 BHO, 'Parishes: Great Gaddesden' in *A History of the County of Hertford*, Vol. 2 ed. William Page (London, 1908). *https://www.british-history.ac.uk/vch/herts/vol2/pp201-207* [accessed 25 June 2020].

Edward relinquished his throne and was deposed. Both Hughes were direct ancestors of Alice le Despenser, who married John IV Dudley de Sutton 3rd (1361-1396). John and Alice were 18th generation ancestors in this saga. It was not John IV's lot to be the next Dudley baron but his son John became Sutton 4th, Dudley 18th.

The Despensers are in Danny Dyer's tree too.[66] Danny learnt that Edward II was dominated by his male favourites and of the rumours of the King's intense, exclusive relationships. Danny visited Leeds Castle, Kent, where he rowed on the moat with serene swans for company. Landing by the castle he found an awaiting historian, who explained that Edward II was a people person, liking commoners, but he and Isabella became a dysfunctional couple. Danny experienced an *Eastenders* moment. Queen Isabella was a vivid, interesting, medieval woman. She was strong and took political action in company with Roger de Mortimer. Not called 'She Wolf' without reason, Isabella would have chopped off Hugh the Younger's penis and tossed it into the fire without hesitation. Castration was rare but Isabella was vengeful.

As an aside, Danny Dyer murmured "Bless you" to Louis IX and called him "Grand-pa". The sainted King was Danny's 26 x great-grandfather. Louis IX had made a new paradise ready for Christ's return to His throne on Earth in the cathedral.[67] The Pope sainted him 27 years after his death in 1270. Louis X (1289-1316), brother of Edward II Plantagenet, was a first cousin-in-law in this saga: many, many times removed (19 generations' wife's great-great-uncle).

Thomas Ligon (1623-1675) was Courteney Cox's great x 9 paternal grandfather, who sailed to Virginia, America from Warwickshire. She found out with astonishment that Berkeley Castle in Gloucestershire was built by Thomas de Berkeley, her great x 18 grandfather on Ligon's line. Farming land in Gloucestershire was fertile and profitable. She was told that Thomas had held Edward II prisoner there in 1327. Danny was locked into the actual cell at Berkeley Castle where Edward had been held and made to resign his throne. An unbearable stench would have risen from a dungeon below. Edward's end came when, as the story was told to Danny, he was smothered with feather beds in the night and a trumpet was put up his fundament, to which act Danny uttered,

---

66 'Who Do You Think You Are? Danny Dyer', BBC (online), (Series 13), (15 November 2016). *https://www.bbc.co.uk/programmes/p04gfg0l* (accessed 3 August 2020).

67 'Danny Dyer…', YouTube videos. *https://www.YouTube.com* [accessed 31 July 2020].

"Like a soap opera? Lovers' triangles?"

After a considered pause,

"Glad there's no trumpet round about."

Edward III – reigned 1327-1377

Edward was crowned in February 1327. Mortimer's Hole is reputed to be the route by which Edward III's troops entered Nottingham Castle to capture Roger de Mortimer in 1330. The King suspected Mortimer of being involved in his father Edward II's murder. Mortimer was hanged at the Tower on 29 November. Archaeologists found the origin of the real tunnel to be on Park Estate not Brewhouse Yard as previously thought, a discovery made in 2010 during a Nottingham Cave Survey.[68]

Courteney Cox's previous next 19th generation earlier was Roger Mortimer, who basically ruled England and got so close to Queen Isabella. Without a proper trial, Roger's guilt was assumed and his voice silenced by being gagged while bound, he was drawn and hanged whereas Thomas de Berkeley was acquitted. Hugh Despenser was another great x 18 grandfather of Courteney's.[69]

What does this have to do with the Sutton Dudleys? The first wife of John IV Dudley de Sutton 3rd, was Alice (born le Despenser) a descendant of Hugh the Elder. For those wondering who Dudley's 15th Baron was, Hugh the Younger had usurped the Dudley barony 1325-1326 yet may never have visited the castle. However, archaeologists found a tile showing the coat of arms of Botiller, who was his castle warden from Tewkesbury.[70] [71]

Ralph de Stafford, 22 generations direct ancestor, father of Catherine (Katherine), helped Edward III take the throne. His own father Edmund de Stafford had been a tenant-in-chief. The King raised Ralph to Earl of Stafford

---

68 *'Real' Mortimer's Hole uncovered by Cave Survey*, BBC Nottingham (2010). *http://news.bbc.co.uk/local/nottingham/hi/people_and_places/history/newsid_9179000/9179392.stm*

69 'Who Do You Think You Are? *The Guardian*, USA review – the one where Monica goes in search of her ancestors', *The Guardian* (20 March 2018).

70 *Encyclopaedia Britannica*, eds., 'Edward II King of England (Edward of Caernarvon)'. *https://www.britannica.com/biography/Edward-II-king-of-England#ref28476* [accessed 1 July 2020].

71 J. Hemingway, *An illustrated chronicle of the castle and Barony of Dudley*, pp.47-48. All Rights Reserved.

in 1350. Ralph's wife Margaret (b. de Audley) was worth £2,314 yearly, she was great-granddaughter of King Edward I by his first Consort, Eleanor of Castille. Ralph abducted her and they married in 1336.[72]

There were many Dudley Johns. The 16th Dudley Baron was John II de Sutton 1st, who also became Lord of Malpas and Shocklech in 1329. Many lands were given to this John by his father Richard (unknown), who had received them from Edward III, presumably a sign of this man's good reputation with the King. A Richard de Turhill of Sedgley is thought to have been one of John's tenants.[73] The name Turley is relevant later in this saga. Turle's land is noteworthy in relation to them and Turl's Hill was a small estate with much history. It was originally within the Township of Ettingshall, Sedgley, to the north east, while simultaneously being in the parish and manor of Sedgley. A good example of how the three institutions of manor, church and vill could work in harness. Livestock was the most likely form of medieval farming given that land was mostly of meadow and pasture. Turl's Hill became part of the Township of Woodsetton in post-medieval times.[74] In an early reference from 1272, John of Terhull was mentioned in an Inquisition Post Mortem on the death of Roger de Somery, Lord Dudley. The services the lord expected from John were ploughing, haymaking and reaping in the lord's demesne. Also, he was required to carry wood probably from Old Park to Dudley Castle for Christmas use. These tasks suggest that this John was a free farmer. A further Inquisition document dated 1292 concerned Roger de Terhull, who was a vendor of wood in Baggeridge and the Haye. Turls Hill House was demolished in the 20th century.

By 1346 John was fighting under the Malpas Cross at the Battle of Crecy.[75] He was in France again in 1350 at St. Jean D'Angley and took part in the Siege of Calais in July 1347. When John died, his wife Isabella held the 17th barony from 1360 until 1397. She remarried, to Richard Fisscher of Dudley, and it was her grandson John IV de Sutton 3rd who inherited all, including Dudley Castle.

---

72 Kathryn Warner, *Edward II: Welcome to the site which examines the events, issues and personalities of Edward II's reign 1307-1327.* 'The de Clare Lands' (posted 29 November 2013). *https://edwardthesecond.blogspot.com/p/my-publications.html* [accessed 2 July 2020].

73 Edward Chitham, *The Story of Dudley*, p.56.

74 Dudley Metropolitan, 'Woodsetton Township'.

75 William Salt Library, Wrottesley, 'Crecy to Calais', vol. xviii.

Interestingly, the wife of Edward Dudley Baron 21st was Cecily (b. Willoughby).[76] She was a descendant of King Edward III on the line of her mother Catherine Neville 1401-1478, upward to John of Gaunt with Katherine Swynford Roet, direct ancestors-in-law of this saga. John of Gaunt was King Edward's eldest surviving son when Richard II came to the throne. After Edward's long reign, his death brought much chaos. Cecily had Greys and Woodvilles in her family tree plus several powerful names on her maternal side:

> Aleida Holland (1226-1283), child of Jean de Avesnes II, Count of Hainaut (1247-1304);
>
> Philippina, Countess of Luxembourg Maas (1252-1311), her father Charles II de Anjou;
>
> Marguerite, Princess of Sicily & Naples (1273-1299).

On paper the marriage between Edward and Cecily seems very shrewd indeed.

Other ancestry surnames are significant later in this saga: Turls lands, All Saints Church (Persehouse family) and Cotwallend (Elwells). Sedgley vill was tiny, considering it was in a very large parish consisting of a number of place names: Turls Hill in the east, Gornal in the south, Gospel End in the west and Sedgley and Ettingshall Woods in the north east. Subsequent settlement along Cotwallend Lane and south of it was probably late medieval or post-medieval.

The Hundred Years' War (1337-1453) saw the rise of unpopular lords, who were big spenders. The Black Death of 1349 would have been sudden and shocking, Midlands people suffered terribly, in Halesowen 40% of adult males died.[77] It is likely that John III de Sutton 2nd was fighting at the Battle of Crecy and was recalled to Parliament, following which he returned to France during 1350. It is possible that he missed exposure to the Black

---

76 Darren Lythgoe, 'Cecily Willoughby (1463-1539)', *Montgomery and Rowntree Families and Genealogy* (2001-2020). *http://strongfamilytree.org/showsource.php?sourceID=S1209&tree=STR06* [accessed 24 June 2020].

77 Zvi Razi, *Life, Marriage and Death in a Medieval Parish: Economy, Society and Demography in Halesowen 1270-1400,* (Cambridge, 1980).

Death. In Dudley there would have been castle stewardship but John possibly added the barbican and chapel block.[78] [79]

In 1347 papal authority was registered:

> "To John de Holande, canon of Chulmelegh. Reservation at the request of queen Philippa of a benefice, value 70 marks with cure of souls, or 44 without, in the gift of the abbess and convent of Shaftesbury notwithstanding that he has the church of prebend of Chulmelegh being 2 marks. He is to resign the church. [see cal. Pet I 110]."[80]

From British History Online sources:[81]

> "John de Trevaur, bishop of St. Asaph. For faculty to make provision to four of his clerks Grante of two apiece. Avignon, Kal. Aug."

> "Ibid., date as above. John de Holande, canon of Chulmelegh and Thomas de Crosse, canon of Crediton, the king's clerks. For plenary remission at the hour of death. Granted."

> "Sir John Cherlecote, son of Alan, had some sort of divorce from his wife Joan. In 1364, he granted Milcote Manor to Thomas, Earl of Warwick."[82]

The father could well have been Alan de Cherleton, who was married to Ellen when Great Gaddesden Manor had been partitioned in 1325.

Sir John would have been a following generation of Cherlecotes (unknown) based on the 1364 date. It does seem that he was receiving private money for praying for souls, a service that could be done for money. He was told to

78 Edward Chitham, *The Story of Dudley*, p.30.

79 John Hemingway, *An illustrated chronicle of the castle and Barony of Dudley 1070-1057*, p.48. All Rights Reserved.

80 Regesta, vol. CLXXV (Regesta, 175): 1346-1347 Calendar of Paper Registers relating to Great Britain and Ireland, vol. 3, 1342-1362. Orig. pub. by HMSO (London, 1897).

81 BHO, 'Vol. XI: 5 Clement VI' in *Petitions to the Pope 1342-1419*, ed. W.H. Bliss. Originally published by Eyre and Spottiswoode (London, 1896), pp.75-76. *https://www.british-history.ac.uk/no-series/petitions-to-pope/1342-1419/pp75-76* [accessed 24 June 2020].

82 BHO, 'Parishes: Weston-upon-Avon with Milcote' in *A History of the County of Warwick: Vol. 5, Kinton Hundred*, ed. L.F. Satzman (London, 1949), pp.198-202. *https://www.british-history.ac.uk/vch/warks/vol5/pp198-202* [accessed 19 June 2020].

resign, this could have been a Catholic reprimand. It is interesting that he was a king's clerk when previous Lord Cherleton(s) had been chamberlains. A relationship between Holande and Cherleton seemed ongoing. Back in 1188, a Courtenay family married into the Okehampton Estates of the Baldwins. John Courtenay appointed a prebend in 1260 to St. Mary Magdalene's, Chulmleigh. This suggests that St. Mary's was indeed a private place of worship, which meant that clerics could then be appointed as wished and so the church was not a normal parish church but a collegiate church under a rector and five prebends, who were not necessarily ordained priests – such a post could be a sinecure.[83]

Most of the powerful families on both sides in the Wars of the Roses were Marcher Lords, feudal aristocrats in the bounding land between the West Midlands and Wales. Most had ancestral connections with Welsh Royal Houses. Henry Tudor claimed descent from Princes of Gwynedd and Princes of Powys. Genuine Welsh people with the surname Powis who did well on English soil are connected to the Cowper-Powyses.[84]

Richard II – reigned 1377-1399

Funding the Hundred Years' War from the public purse caused civil unrest; society was already impoverished following the Black Death, more so as defeats against the French had left England weak.[85] Real power lay with Richard's uncle, John of Gaunt, yet Richard II is well-known for his handling of the Peasant's Revolt of 1381. He did quite well given his youth. More relevant here is the forthcoming dynastic turmoil that Richard faced. It ended with his abdication. This was a power struggle against barons, as many leading magnates had their own private armies. Risking resentment from others, Richard favoured Michael de la Pole, his chancellor. Power bypassed the King because of the formation of a 'Council of Government' run by 'Lords Apellants', who were the five most senior magnates. Of the five, Bolingbroke, John of Gaunt's son, usurped the throne to become Henry IV.[86]

---

83 Britain Express: Passionate about Heritage, "Chulmleigh, St Mary Magdalene Church", ed. David Ross, (n.d.). *https://britainexpress.com* [accessed 6 August 2020].

84 Mick Powis, *Powis Pages: The People of the Rural Area. A History of the Powis Family*, trudy. weaver@myself.com. All Rights Reserved.

85 The Finer Times, "Wars of the Roses". *https://www.thefinertimes.com/wars-of-the-roses* [accessed 22 April 2020].

86 *Kings and Queens*, pp.94-95.

Chapter 3

Battling Roses?

YORKIST AND Lancastrian rivals battled over the crown in the Wars of the Roses, a series of civil wars. Henry IV was a descendant of Edward III, whose youngest son was John de Gaunt, Duke of Lancaster, hence Lancastrian red rose (the Percy family, for example, were inclined towards the Lancastrian side).[87] The 3rd son was the Duke of York, Yorkist white rose. The rose names of the wars represented their crests and certainties of entitlement to the English crown. Trouble bubbled in the two factions for years before conflict broke out. For complicated reasons, the Percys and the Nevilles were enemies after 1453. At this stage, the saga is mainly about the Sutton Dudleys, most of whom were direct ancestors. Their lives were set dangerously close to powerful families, including royals, dangerous because executions were a real threat, sometimes carelessly proclaimed after hearing a whisper. The Wars of the Roses were gradually approaching.

Historians concentrate on the decline of towns in the period after the Black Death of 1349 and especially in the 1400s. The deaths would have been sudden and shocking. In Staffordshire, houses and plots of land lacked tenants, buildings fell into ruin, shops needed repair and holdings of land were amalgamated. As building costs were normally met by the tenant, the lord's circumstances were compromised. Population of the countryside generally declined more than in towns, the consequences were gradual and

---

87 The History Jar: English History from 1066, 'Henry Percy, Fourth Earl of Northumberland'. *https://thehistoryjar.com* [accessed 8 June 2020].

individuals needed to be flexible. Adaptable individuals who were survivors and their descendants, after the Black Death, enjoyed greater prosperity in the 1400s. Peasants held larger acreages, switching from arable to pasture for higher prices and lower labour costs while unskilled wage earners were paid 4d per day instead of 1d-2d before the plague.[88] After the Black Death country people could afford better food, especially quantities of meat, which helped explain the large numbers of butchers in the 1400s. Country people reaped the rewards whereas lords faced difficult problems, less easy for big egos. Worse still, they endured hard times emotionally as well as financially. Economists have learnt to recognise patterns in various periods of slump and boom, similar past episodes with similar knock-on effects help to make considered predictions feasible.

After the great Peasant's Revolt of 1381, serfdom and villeinage slowly gave way to money rent transactions, which enabled former peasants to rise to yeomen status. By the 15th century, such folk merged into the gentry class, to an extent that displaced the power of nobles. Loyalties could easily shift and die in what was called 'bastard feudalism', an unstable system which could enrage magnates confronted with social change. These troubles brought the circumstances that led up to the Wars of the Roses.

Henry IV – reigned 1399-1413

When Henry Plantagenet became King in 1399 he merged the Lincoln title with his Lancastrian title, Great Gaddesden Manor was settled on Longespee heirs, Ela and her husband Roger la Zouche.[89] Significant to the ancestry in question, another repository with content from 1401 onwards included Sutton entries, findable via Hull University Archives.[90]

Sir Payn Tiptoft (alt. Typotot) had been on a jaunt with John of Gaunt, trudging from Calais to Bordeaux. He became an entrusted retainer of the

88 'The Urbanization of Staffordshire: The First Phases (1)', Christopher Dyer, lecture given at the 21st Earl Lecture, University of Keele, 9 November 2001, *Staffordshire Studies*, 14 (2002).

89 BHO, Parishes: 'Great Gaddesden' in *A History of the County of Hertford*: Vol. 2, ed. William Page (London, 1908), pp.201-207.

90 University of Hull Archives, Ref. UDDBA, Papers of the Barnard Family of South Cave, collection, forms a repository (1401-1911). Ref. L.9.64SU. Includes Sutton: a Sutton bibliography, sources of local history information about Sutton on Hull / compiled by Patricia Cassidy (1991). Ref. L.728.8. The History and People of Netherhall (formely known as Sutton Hall), date unknown.

Lords Appellant, siding with Gloucester and Warwick (d.1439). He even managed to obtain a royal pardon when Arundel was executed. Next he served Henry IV as a henchman and was called to military service to put down a Percy rebellion in the north of England. Tiptoft was an MP and his children included John Tiptoft, Earl of Worcester, and Joyce Tiptoft (b.1430) wife of Edmund Sutton (b.1425).[91]

Henry V – reigned 1413-1422

Kingston Ford's lectures were based on a neutral survey of the narrative sources of the 15th century.[92] Other modern unbiased sources were provided by McFarlane and his pupils, who studied less the way landowners depended on maintaining their retainers and tenants and more on lower landowners of the 15th century, the gentry. Personal letters of the Paston gentry family were researched by Gairdner and also Davis. Gentry families, such as Stonor, Cely and others wrote insightful letters too. An example of a family that rose from humble origins was the Catesbies of Coventry. Gentry in their localities were important to the politics of the age, however, dynastic conflicts interested them less than their own lands and fortunes.

There was much switching of loyalties during the Wars of the Roses because, basically, it was a great royal and noble family squabble of power-hungry similar relations. To the players it was known as 'the Cousins War'. Though related to the York standard bearers in the 'Wars of Succession' (another name for the wars), Margaret Beaufort was closely related to and aligned with the Lancastrian party as well. Henry VI was her brother-in-law through her marriage to Edmund Tudor. Margaret Beaufort's second marriage to Sir Henry Stafford, younger son of the Duke of Buckingham, Humphrey Stafford (another descendant of Edward III) was far from diverse. It required a papal dispensation for the couple to marry because they were

---

91 L.S. Woodger, 'Tiptoft, Sir Payne (1351-1413) of Burwell, Cambs.' In *The History of Parliament: The House of Commons 1386-1421,* ed. J.S. Roskell, et al. (1993). *http://www.historyofparliament online.org/volume/1386-1421/member/tiptoft-sir-payn-1351-1413* [accessed 27 June 2020].

92 Bruce Webster, *The Wars of the Roses* (Pennsylvania, 1900, London, 1998), maps, pp.7-8, 11-13, 42, 44. C.L. Kingsford, *Prejudice and Promise in Fifteenth Century England* (Oxford, 1925). (Unseen). K.B. McFarlane, *England in the Fifteenth Century* (London, 1981). (Unseen). *The Paston Letters*, ed. Gairdner (1904), 6 vols. Microprint ed. vol. 1 (Gloucester, 1983). (Unseen). Paston Letters and Papers of the Fifteenth Century (Oxford, 1971-1976), (2 parts, unseen).

so closely related to each other.[93] However, there was no issue from their marriage.

Henry VI first reigned 1422-1461

Six years into Henry VI's reign, Joan of Arc rallied French armies against the English. The Hundred Years' War with France initiated a new lay subsidy to be taxed, which in Dudley brought about the compilation of a revised list of inhabitants containing 42 names. This raised 76s 8d for the war effort. Ricardus Frebody had inherited his family holding, Petrus le Fleshewar's name suggests that the borough was concerned with the quality of meat in the market.[94] Towns like Dudley, in general, took little part in provoking civil war and disturbance.

Dynastic turmoil within England was to reduce the English threat to France. By 1437 it was apparent that Lancastrian Henry VI was ill-equipped for late medieval kingship, his poor mental health raised problems. His Queen, Margaret of Anjou, had five attendants, including direct saga ancestors Dame Elizabeth Grey, eldest daughter of Sir Richard Woodville (alt. Wydville) and his wife Jacquetta of Luxembourg, Duchess of Bedford. The Woodvilles were an old Northamptonshire family said to be descended from a Norman called William de Wydville.[95] When 18th generation Elizabeth (born Woodville) was at court, her first husband, Sir John Grey, was one of the Queen's captains. Suffolk and his wife conveyed the manor of Grafton, held of the King as of the honor of Pinkney, valued at £24 a year, to Richard and Jacquetta.

The final collapse of the attempt to conquer France, which had dominated English policy for so long, aroused shame and fury against those who might be held responsible by the 1450s. In London, power became concentrated in the hands of a narrow clique of ambitious magnates: initially the Duke of Suffolk followed by the Duke of Somerset. Both were supported by Henry VI's wife Margaret, who was aggressive and fearless in excluding other increasingly bitter members of government, themselves aware of the power vacuum.[96]

---

93 John Johnson Lewis, *Margaret Beaufort Biography*, ThoughtCo, (updated 3 July 2019). *https://www.thoughtco.com/margaret-beaufort-tudo-dynasty-3530617* [accessed 19 April 2020].

94 Edward Chitham, *The Story of Dudley* (Stroud, 2014), p.29.

95 Alison Weir, *Lancaster and York: The Wars of the Roses* (London, 1995), p.324.

96 *Kings and Queens of the British Isles*, ed. Thomas Cussans, *The Times* (London, 2015), pp.106 107, illus., maps.

In Kent, so-called 'lesser men' with roles such as sheriff, under-sheriff, gaol keeper (as well as higher status esquire, steward and constable) monopolised powerful positions. Their extortions, false imprisonments and violent outrages were listed in the indictments before and after Jack Cade's rebellion of 1450. The most known rebel was Cade of Kent.[97]

John V de Sutton 4th Dudley 18th was married to Constance Blount, daughter of red-headed Sir Walter le Blount, who had been killed at the Battle of Shrewsbury in 1403 and was immortalised by Shakespeare. Constance developed Himley Hall as an alternative home to Dudley Castle. Walter carried the Royal Standard for Henry IV and was killed by Archibald, 4th Earl of Douglas on Henry Hotspur's rebel side. The Blounts then found they had a stake in John V's fortune as his mother-in-law, Sancha de Toledo-Alaya, took custody of his six-year-old first son (John VI), heir to his valuable Dudley Estates.[98] [99] Constance held the Dudley 19th barony title until she died in 1432.

Some historians point to specific economic problems around 1450, especially the collapse of wool exports as that caused much hardship to previously prosperous sheep-farmers and merchants. The wine trade suffered likewise. Social consequences of the Black Death, as well as further high mortality due to recurrent plagues, meant surviving tenants' relationships with landlords improved but fewer tenants meant less farming manpower for lords.

22 May 1455, First Battle of St. Albans, Royalist Defeat

This battle marked the start of the Wars of the Roses. The Royals were commanded by Edmund Beaufort, who was killed. On the other side was Richard, Duke of York, Richard Neville of Warwick and his father, the Earl of Salisbury. As previously mentioned, there were complicated reasons why the Percys and the Nevilles were enemies after 1453. Direct 19 generations ancestor of this saga, John Dudley Baron 20th, was hit by an arrow in his

---

97 Bruce Webster, *The Wars of the Roses*, pp.41, 60-61. I.M.W. Harvey, *Jack Cade's Rebellion of 1450* (Oxford, 1991). (Unseen).

98 William Ryland Beall, et al., Ancestral Roots of Certain American Colonists who Came to America Before 1700 (2004), p.85.

99 'Ulster Genealogical and Historical Guild' ed. Kenneth Darwin, *Familia: Ulster Genealogical Review* (1990), p.26. (Belfast: Ulster Historical Foundation).

face.[100] The battle was a Lancastrian defeat, magnates versus government. Margaret of Anjou and her son, Prince Edward of Westminster, the Prince of Wales, fled in exile. The next big battle would be at Northampton but there were skirmishes and minor battles in between at Blore Heath and Ludford Bridge.

Magnates, gentry, yeomen, tenant farmers, fishermen, town dwellers and itinerant folk saw much character and diversity about them yet unless individuals were retainers, soldiers, or they dwelled near battle sites such as St. Albans, the Wars of the Roses hardly touched England's population.

23 September 1459, Battle of Blore Heath, Yorkist Victory

John Dudley 20th Baron was again wounded and captured, however, Henry made him a Knight of the Garter.

The Parr family came from Lancashire.[101] Sir William Parr's maternal grandparents were Sir Thomas Tunstall and Isabel Harington, a granddaughter of Sir Thomas Stanley, 1st Earl of Derby.[102] Cecily, 7th Baroness Harington (born Bonville), was a 17th generation direct ancestor of this saga. In the following century, there were further intermarriages between Dudley Sutton barons and the Haringtons, Greys and Stanleys.

Lady Eleanor Butler (born Talbot) was daughter to the Earl of Shrewsbury and Margaret Beauchamp, and at age 13 she entered an arranged marriage to Sir Thomas Butler, son and heir of Lancastrian Lord Sudeley. It is thought Sir Thomas Butler died in 1461 but before the Battle of Towton, this is mentioned because another Thomas Butler died on the Lancastrian side in that battle. As a widow, Eleanor would have been a likely choice if there was a prior betrothal before Elizabeth Woodville's marriage to Edward. However, Ashdown-Hill noted that the 'Inquisition Post Mortem' was dated to Henry VI's reign not Edward IV's.[103] Alternatively, had Sir Thomas Butler died at the Battle of Blore Heath in 1459, Eleanor would have been a wealthier widow than she seemed.

---

100 John Hemingway, *An Illustrated Chronicle of the Cluniac Priory of St. James, Dudley* (Dudley, 2005), p.66.

101 Linda Porter, *Katherine, the Queen; the Remarkable Life of Katherine Parr* (Macmillan, 2010).

102 Douglas Richardson, *Magna Carta Ancestry: A Study in Colonial and Medieval Families*, 2nd ed (2006), pp.206-207.

103 Public Records Office, *Inquisitions Post Mortem* (formerly known as escheal probate). (London, 2019). *https://publicrecordsearch.co.uk/england* [accessed 18 June 2020].

There are several similarities between Eleanor and Elizabeth Woodville's circumstances. Edward attempted to bribe Elizabeth's father and threatened violence. His next ploy could have been to offer marriage to Elizabeth. Three years earlier if he had pre-contracted Eleanor, he would have been that much younger and more naïve. If Edward had a secret wife already, it could be another explanation for his behaviour. Ashdown-Hill speculated that Edward's promise to Eleanor happened just after his coronation.[104] Much of the evidence relating to Edward's prior marriage to another woman is circumstantial and the sources biased. Sir Thomas More thought Edward was pre-contracted with Elizabeth Lucy Wayte and furthermore believed they had two children together, while Wagner noticed that Margaret of Anjou and the Lancastrians made no reference to any pre-existing marriage.

According to Jayne Vautour (online spelling), "whatever the revisionists" said, Edward would not have needed a promise of marriage with Eleanor, all he had to do was reinstate her lands. Jayne posted how Richard "made the whole thing up." Eleanor had herself found the confidence to petition Edward for the return of manors. On the other hand, Sir Kevin Parr specifically believed that the "good lady" who died in "that nunnery" was Edward's true wife, implying they were married by Stephen the priest and understanding that the Butler family keep a treasured statement in which the bride is wrongly named Eliz not Elen.

1459, Battle of Ludford Bridge

Ludford Bridge crosses the River Teme, Shropshire: on the north bank lies Ludlow where the town occupied a bend in the river. At dawn on 13 October, the Yorkist troops knelt in submission before King Henry and received his pardon. The King and his army returned to Coventry where a Parliament attainted York, Salisbury and Warwick.[105]

---

104 The History Jar: English History from 1066, *'Eleanor Butler – the holiest harlot or an unrecognised Queen'*, posted by JuliaH, (21 January 2016). *https://thehistoryjar.com* [accessed 24 March 2019]. Contributers include Susan Abermethy and Sir Kevin Parr, Bt. Ashdown-Hill, *Eleanor the Secret Queen: the Woman who put Richard III on the Throne* (Stroud, The History Press, 2010).

105 *English Monarchs*, 'The Battle of Ludford Bridge 12 October 1459'. *https://www.englishmonarchs.co.uk/battle_of_ludford_bridge.html* [accessed 4 June 2020].

10 July 1460, Battle of Northampton, Yorkist Victory

Warwick (future Kingmaker) with Salisbury, his father, and Edward (future Edward IV) sailed from France and landed at Sandwich enroute to London. It was during the ensuing battle that Lord Grey, a commander in the King's army, switched allegiance to the Yorkist cause, which helped the outcome of the battle as the King's side lost. Henry VI was captured, which badly affected his mental health and caused permission to be granted for Richard to be England's Regent. Meanwhile Margaret of Anjou was planning to create an army in Wales.

Late in November 1460, at Sandal Castle, Queen Margaret was happy to allow her army to sack the homes of the tenants of York and Salisbury. Lancastrians noted that no herons had nested in the adjacent park that year (superstition was widespread at a level that seems ridiculous today). York and Salisbury marched north in December: by pressing to York's summons, Lord Neville then deserted to the Lancastrians.[106]

30 December 1460, Battle of Wakefield, Lancastrian Victory

This victory cost Richard his life, 3rd Duke of York, father of Edward, Earl of March, aged 19 (who would be crowned). Richard had made bad decisions and should have won the battle. Salisbury and another son of York's were captured and later executed. As Richard of York had died, Edward IV was anointed King of England in March 1461.

Edward IV – reigned 1461-1471 for the first part of his monarchy

Edward IV was to raise Richard Woodville's title to 1st Earl Rivers in 1466. Previously the Woodvilles seem to have been living at Grafton, presumably sometime tenants of the de Poles.[107]

2 February 1461, Battle of Mortimer's Cross, Yorkist Victory

The Earl of March was now the new Duke of York. Lord Grey of Wilton and Humphrey Stafford were among his supporters, based at Wigmore Castle

106 Alison Weir, *Lancaster and York, The Wars of the Roses*, (London, 1995), pp.253-254, illus.

107 BHO, 'Grafton Regis' in *A History of the County of Northampton*: Vol. 5, *The Hundred of Cleley*, ed. Philip Riden and Charles Insley (London, orig. pub. by Victoria County History, 2002), pp.142-176. *https://www.british-history.ac.uk/vch/northants/vols/pp142-176* [accessed 3 June 2020]. Fn. 113 Baker, Northants, ii. 161-163, *Complete Peerage*, xi. 15-7.

near the Welsh border and Lugg River. A meteorological phenomenon known as 'parhelion' or 'sun dog' occurred due to a very rare atmospheric illusion when three suns visibly rise. Edward calmed the ensuing hysteria by telling his troops that the trio represented the Holy Trinity. Quite quick thinking, that. Later his emblem became 'Sun in splendour', representing the three surviving sons of York: himself, Richard and George. The event was dramatised in Shakespeare's *Henry VI, part 3*. That misty morning, Richard Devereux led the Yorkist right, the Earl of Pembroke commanded the left. Owen Tudor, grandfather of Henry VII, was taken prisoner and subsequently beheaded in Hereford. His head was set on the market cross.[108]

Storey described what happened in Lincolnshire in 1461:

> "The tide of civil warfare in 15th century England only twice touched the county of Lincoln. Queen Margaret passed through in January 1461, covering the land – according to a monk of Croyland – over a breadth of 30 miles as they pillaged and... plundered. Grantham and Stamford were sacked but it is unlikely that these uncontrollable followers of the Lancastrian Queen penetrated the shire much beyond its south-west corner."[109] [110]

They stampeded in flight from the approach of Edward IV:

> "... the local chronicler has nothing to say of their passage other than that they were compelled to abandon their booty."

17 February 1461, Second Battle of St Albans, Yorkists Victory

Elizabeth Woodville was widowed when Lancastrian Sir John Grey of Groby was killed in this 2nd Battle of St. Albans. Cecily, 7th Baroness of Harington, to be Grey of Groby (born Bonville and at age one in 1461) was to be

---

108 *English Monarchs*, 'The Battle of Mortimers Cross 2 February 1461'. *https://www.englishmonarchs.co.uk/battle_of_mortimers_cross.html* [accessed 4 June 2020]. William Shakespeare, *Henry VI, part 3* (circa 1591).

109 R.L. Storer, in *Nottingham Medieval Studies*, vol. 14, pp.64-83 (Brepols Publishers, 2020). *https://www.brepolsonline.net/doi/abs/10.1484/J.NMS.3.47?journalCode=nms* [accessed 22 April 2020].

110 Society in Lincoln Guildhall on 27 September 1969. Fn. 2 Rerum Anglicarum Sciptorum Veterum, ed. W. Fulman, vol. 1, pp.531-532 (Oxford, 1684).

the richest heiress in England after her male relatives were slain in battles against Lancastrians. As a young widow, Elizabeth would marry Edward IV and be Queen Consort, crossing from Lancastrian to Yorkist loyalty. She was grandmother to John Dudley, who was 22nd Baron, only until 1537 because misfortune caused him to be disgraced by poverty and called 'Lord Quondam'.

27-28 March 1461, Battle of Ferrybridge, Yorkist Victory

Only one day before Towton, the Yorkists forced their way across the River Aire at Ferrybridge, defeating the Lancastrians' attempt to hold the line of the river. There are two different accounts, one from *Hall's Chronicle* and one from *Waurin's Chronicle*. Also there were George Neville's vague letters from nearer the time. Accounts agree that Edward took and crossed the bridge.[111]

29 March 1461, Battle of Towton, Yorkist Victory

Two further battles were fought where Yorkists were able to annihilate the Lancastrians. Yorkists remained in power for the next decade of relative peace. William, Sir Lord Hastings of Kirby Muxloe Castle in Leicestershire, was knighted by Edward IV in the aftermath of Towton and became chamberlain to the King's household. As a courtier he helped arrange the marriage of Margaret of York, Edward's sister, to the Duke of Burgundy. Mancini described Hastings as being privy to all of Edward's pleasures.

25 April 1464, Battle of Hedgeley Moor, Northumberland, Yorkist Victory

James III of Scotland strongly supported Margaret of Anjou. From his court she gathered forces to invade England. Now Henry Beaufort, Duke of Somerset, had made peace with Edward IV and had been pardoned by him, his estates were restored. Nevertheless, he defected again to Henry and Margaret's cause: he met up with other pardoned Lancastrian nobles and after Christmas failed to ambush John Neville near Newcastle (then named Marquess of Montagu not Earl of Northumberland). Beaufort and Neville faced each other at Hedgeley. Nobles, such as Sir Ralph Grey, Sir Ralph Percy

111 J. Richard, *Battle of Ferrybridge*, 27-28 March 1461 (2 December 2013). *http://www.historyofwar.org/articles/battles_ferrybridge.html* [accessed 5 June 2020] *Hall's Chronicle*. *Waurin's Chronicle*. George Neville, *Letters*.

and Lord Roos were with the Lancastrians. Percy was notorious by this time for constantly changing sides. When it came to it, the Rooses flew from the battle before it began. Consequently, most Lancastrians followed their flight in panic. Percy fell to his death from his horse because the alarmed animal's leap was as magnified as a fisherman's biggest catch, 'Percy's Cross' marks the unfortunate site. Edward IV managed to achieve James III's envoys' safe passage from Scotland to York for peace negotiations.[112]

Elizabeth Woodville Grey and Edward secretly married on May Day 1464 in a hermitage, thought to be a small chapel in the woods, near the manor house occupied by the Woodvilles since 1440 in 'Grafton Woodville' Northants.[113]

14 May 1464, Battle of Hexham, Yorkist Victory

Lancastrian defeat at Hedgeley Moor did not deter the Lancastrians; they tried and lost again less than a month later outside Hexham.

As Queen Consort to Edward, Elizabeth was crowned by Archbishop Bourchier on Whitsunday 1465 in a splendid ceremony at Westminster Abbey. During Edward IV's reign, he and Elizabeth repossessed a chantry in Grafton that had been neglected by St. James's Abbey, Northampton. This could have been where their marriage took place and they may have also used it as a private chapel. It was to be subject to dissolution in 1538. There was earlier evidence of the chantry having been a hermitage at Grafton between 1180-1205. In 1483, Earl Rivers made a will leaving money to recruit a new priest for the hermitage, also the last Earl Rivers (3rd) mentioned 'the old inheritance' he held therein.

Dockray cited one chronicler, John Warkworth, who wrote in the 1460s:

> "When King Edward reigned [there was] much trouble and great loss of goods among the common people, as first the 15th of all their goods, and then a whole 15th [a reference to Edward IV's taxation]."[114]

---

112 *English Monarchs,* 'The Battle of Hedgeley Moor 25 April 1464'. *https://www.englishmonarchs.co.uk/battle_of_hedgeley_moor.html* [accessed 4 June 2020].

113 BHO, 'Grafton Regis'. Fn. 19 *P.N. Northants.*, 99; below, manors and other estates. Fn. 64 N.R.O., Fermor-Hesketh, F/30/2. Fn. 69 N.R.O., Fermor-Hesketh, F/7/2-3; Parker, 'Medieval Hermitage', p.251.

114 Bruce Webster, *The Wars of the Roses*, pp.44, 66-67. John Warkworth (1460s) cited from 'Three Chronicles of the Reign of Edward IV, with an Introduction by Keith Dockray', ed. K. Dockray, (Gloucester, 1988), p.34. (Unseen). C. Carpenter, *Locality and Polity: a Study of Warwickshire Landed Society, 1401-1499* (Cambridge, 1992), pp.481-486, 559. (Unseen).

After he married into the Woodville family, Edward began to find his Neville relations irksome.[115] Lord Warwick had not been consulted about Edward's secret marriage and was critical of Edward's choice of bride, regarding her to be of low birth which was a slight to her mother, the Duchess of Bedford, Jacquetta of Luxembourg, whose parents were Count Peter of Luxembourg (and his wife Margaret, born de Baux).

Jacquetta was hardly a commoner but she had been accused of it previously. Aged 19, Jacquetta had been the widow of Henry V's brother, John of Lancaster, with whom she spent two years in a childless marriage. Elizabeth's father, Richard Woodville was John's chamberlain and accompanied her back to England from Normandy. A relationship began between them, which culminated in wedlock. Their marriage caused a scandal as Richard was considered to be a commoner and Henry VI fined Richard £1,000 for failing to obtain his permission to marry.[116] *The Guardian* printed a medieval historian's critique of the BBC historical drama.[117] Elizabeth Woodville is remembered as 'The White Queen', Margaret Beaufort as 'The Red Queen'.

Elizabeth Woodville, drawing by Katherine Wiseman.

Eleanor Butler might have given the impression that she had few people to protect her and was a poorer widow than Elizabeth Woodville Grey had been. However, this was false. Eleanor's sister, the Duchess of Norfolk, was related to the Beauchamps. Her uncle, Earl Richard Warwick, had good reason not to speak of a pre-marriage because while the Queen Consort was being

115 The History Jar: English History from 1066, 'Henry Percy, Fourth Earl of Northumberland'.

116 BBC, *Jacquetta Woodville. https://www.bbc.co.uk/programming/profiles/1J1RkP4VorsW7mWvy HC70KX/Jacquetta-Woodville* [accessed 27 April 2020].

117 'A Medieval Historian's View of the White Queen. Professor Michael Hicks interviewed by Laura Barnett', *The Guardian* (24 June 2013). *https://www.theguardian.com/.../24/medieval historians-view-white-queen* [accessed 1 May 2020].

introduced to court, he was in France negotiating a marriage for Edward to French Princess, King Louis XI's relative, Bona of Savoy.[118] At the time of the Wars of the Roses there was no United Kingdom of course. England's dealings with other countries needed supreme diplomacy, as in the arrangement of lucrative marriages like this one envisaged by Warwick for Edward IV to Bona.

1466 was the year when Edward IV created the title Lord Rivers for Elizabeth's father, who had been a mere mercer and captain of foot to the Duke of York. By 1466 and seen as an imposter, he was made Treasurer of England and was increasingly resented by nobles. Warwick's fury simmered, arguably jealous, he resented Elizabeth Woodville's Lancastrian past, doubted her new loyalties to the house of York and was incensed by how she exploited her position as Queen Consort to advance her Woodvillle family, coupling her brothers and sisters to nobles of rank. He regarded her as a threat to the established order.[119] Edward argued with Warwick over the marriage as well as foreign policy. Was Warwick after power and a major part in parliamentary decision-making? Was his opposition due to ego and pride? Formidable and ambitious, he was particularly angry about issues abroad. Hastings smeared the Woodvilles too, especially Edward IV's step-son Thomas Grey, Earl of Dorset, and Anthony (then Lord Scales).[120] Aristocrats were fickle, many just wanted short-term advantage but their causes resulted in treachery, betrayal and revenge.

When Edward had defeated Henry VI and took the crown from him, Margaret and her son became valuable blue blood property. Edward arranged wardship for young Henry Tudor and a marriage between Henry Stafford's heir and Katherine Woodville, Elizabeth Woodville's sister. This tied the families close together. Margaret and Stafford accepted without protest, consequently they stayed in touch with Margaret's son and even hosted the King in 1468.

26 July 1469, Battle of Edgecote Moor, Lancastrian Victory

Following the defeat of Edward's followers at the Battle of Edgecote Moor, he was taken at Olney but not executed. His Queen Consort Elizabeth had

118 The History Jar: English History from 1066, 'Eleanor Butler – the holiest harlot or an unrecognised Queen'.

119 *Battle of Edgecote Moor, 26th July 1469*, pdf. *https://adelaidegamedesign.weebly.com/uploads/7/8/6/4/78642462/the_battle_of_edgecote_moor.pdf* [accessed 16 April 2016].

120 The History Jar: English History from 1066, 'Kirby Muxloe Castle and William, Lord Hastings', posted by JuliaH, (22 June 2016). *https://thehistoryjar.com* [accessed 24 March 2019]. Contributers include Sir Kevin Parr and Tanguy.

been lodging in the royal apartments at the Tower of London when he was taken into captivity at Warwick Castle. Warwick obtained a pardon for himself with George, 1st Duke of Clarence, and his followers. With the King now his prisoner, he was free to meddle with the social order. Within months he had seized a number of Elizabeth's family. Together, Warwick and Clarence had her father Richard Woodville, 1st Earl Rivers, and her brother Sir John Woodville beheaded without trial at Gosford Green outside the city walls in August 1469. Her older brother Anthony Woodville, now 2nd Earl Rivers, was able to escape.[121] Weir described Anthony and his father as cultivated and talented men, respected abroad as knights of valour and Anthony as kind and just.[122]

Sir Oliver Sutton Dudley died at Edgecote. Lordship was important to the gentry but it was erratic as they would choose to do or not do what their lords asked. Very few of the Warwickshire gentry would support either side in 1460 and 1461 (nor at Bosworth). In 1469, there was no outcry against Warwick and Clarence's talk of "evil advisors" and those "certain sedicious persons", which were mostly aimed at the Woodvilles; neither was there any enthusiasm for Warwick to head government.[123]

People lived in a superstitious age of witch-hunting and wariness of 'the foreign'. A follower of Warwick had produced some images made of lead that he claimed Jacquetta had made for the purposes of witchcraft and sorcery. Despite the fact that her husband and son had then only been recently killed, shock did not prevent her from writing to the mayor and aldermen of London asking for help in refuting the accusations. They assisted, Warwick released Edward from captivity and the King's council cleared her of charges. Jacquetta certainly suffered a personal tragedy when her beloved husband and son were executed by Warwick yet her personal relations with her family were good. It seems that she aided her daughter Elizabeth even though it was by placing a curse on Warwick and his accomplice George (Clarence). However, she consistently courted power and when Warwick had returned to court, she behaved courteously.[124] Reading about Warwick and Clarence, it is easy to imagine them as middle-aged men but the players were relatively young, their juvenile behaviours and lack of maturity are more obvious signs

121 *Battle of Edgecote Moor, 26th July 1469*, pdf.

122 Alison Weir, *Lancaster and York: The Wars of the Roses*, p.324.

123 Bruce Webster, *The Wars of the Roses*, p.28.

124 BBC, *Jacquetta Woodville.*

of youth. Elizabeth Woodville was an acknowledged beauty, Edward truly had been bewitched and spellbound by her.

March 1470, Battle of Losecote Field, Lancastrian Victory

The only skirmish of 1470, the year's events turned against Yorkists and back to Lancastrians.

More from Storer on the second military action in Lincolnshire:

> "Edward descended on the county to rout local rebels at Emperingham, in the skirmish named 'Loose-coat field'. This grand total of two incidents separated by nine years scarcely suggests that Lincolnshire was much disturbed by the Wars of the Roses. The same can be said, however, about most of other English counties."

Great stretches of the country saw nothing of marches or battles, whereas events violent enough to dethrone monarchs impacted public life around the kingdom.[125] Warwick and Clarence were forced to flee to France, where they forged an allegiance with Margaret of Anjou and the French. They could launch their own invasion of England. Meanwhile, Warwick's brother, John Neville, changed from Yorkist to Lancastrian, causing Edward IV to abandon his throne in flight.

Henry VI was re-adepted 1470-1471 but Edward IV was soon restored

Henry VI seized the opportunity and by October 1470 he had reclaimed the throne but only for seven months.[126] Stafford joined the King's forces in putting down rebels, including Margaret Beaufort's relations through her mother's first marriage. After Henry VI was restored to power, she dined with him along with young Henry Tudor and his uncle Jasper Tudor; clearly her alliance was with Lancaster not York. Hastings fled to the continent with Edward. He was cousin by marriage to both brothers, Edward and Richard, Duke of Gloucester (later Richard III), although his wife was Katherine Neville, Warwick's sister.

Descended from the Cherleton's of Powis via her mother, also Joyce, Joyce Tiptoft's brother was previously mentioned – Sir John Tiptoft, 1st Earl of

125 R.L. Storer, in *Nottingham Medieval Studies*, vol. 14, pp.64-83.

126 The Finer Times, 'Wars of the Roses'. *https://www.thefinertimes.com/wars-of-the-roses* [accessed 22 April 2020].

Worcester (8 May 1427-18 October 1470) born at Eversden, Cambridgeshire. As well as being a nobleman, he was also a scholar in Law, Latin and Greek, having studied at University College Oxford and the University of Padua.[127] His steadfast support for York was outstanding through the Wars of the Roses, becoming almost as powerful as Edward IV himself; he had received the Order of the Garter from the King in 1461. Tiptoft's dependability and intellectual ability were impressive assets. He was a devout Catholic, hence his service as emissary to the Pope,[128] even Lancastrians respected him highly, although they also, most probably, spread lies to discredit him. Tiptoft's roles had included Lord High Treasurer, Lord High Constable and Deputy Governor of Ireland. As constable of the Tower of London, he dealt with Lancastrian prisoners, such as Sir Charles Grey; allegedly his punishments could be so dreadful that he was called the 'Butcher of England'. While Henry VI briefly returned to the throne, he had Tiptoft beheaded at the Tower for his Yorkist leanings. Tiptoft's titles became extinct.[129] A cenotaph intended for him at Ely seems to have been used for his son as the earl himself was buried at Blackfriars, Ludgate.

14 April 1471, Battle of Barnet

Warwick's fellow schemers had been King Henry's wife Margaret, who wanted revenge, and Louis XI of France, who supported her. Edward returned to England, bringing Burgundian supporters capable of vicious fighting. George (Clarence) fought for the Yorkists as did Warwick (now the 'Kingmaker') but the latter was killed during this brutal battle in dense fog as was his brother John Neville, who had also changed sides.[130] Sir Thomas Parr's first son, Sir William (1434-1483), along with Sir James Harington had also raised troops to fight at Barnet.[131] [132] [133] The second son married a

---

127 Jonathan Woolfson, *Padua and the Tudors: English Students in Italy 1485-1603* (1998), p.40.

128 Peter Moore and John Horgan, *Welcome to the Worcester Household* (2006). https://*www.worcesterhousehold.co.uk/history.htm* [accessed 27 June 2020]. P141moore@hotmail.com and john@worcesterhousehold.co.uk

129 M.C. Jones, 'Feudal lords of Powys', *Montgomeryshire Collections I* (1868), p.357.

130 The History Jar: English History from 1066, 'Henry Percy, Fourth Earl of Northumberland'.

131 R. Horrox, *Richard III: A Study in Service* (Cambridge, 1989), p.41.

132 C. Ross, *Edward IV* (London, 1975), p.164.

133 R. Horrox, 'Parr, Sir William (1434-1483)', *Oxford Dictionary of National Biography* (Oxford, 2004).

daughter of Sir John Yonge, Lord Mayor of London, the third son was killed at Barnet. Between the Battle of Barnet and the Battle of Tewkesbury, King Henry VI was captured and imprisoned in the Tower of London.

4 May 1471, Battle of Tewkesbury, Yorkist Victory

The Croyland Chronicle (also known as *Crowland*) commented on how well William Hastings was doing, although it was possible he changed allegiance. By now Jane Shaw (alt. Shore) Edward IV's mistress had transferred her affections to Hastings according to Mancini.[134] There was rivalry between Dorset and Hastings concerning Jane Shaw. Royle and other historians of the Wars of the Roses concluded that Richard's accusation that Hastings had been plotting with the Woodvilles via Jane Shaw was near unbelievable. How likely would that be? They already had control of the young King, his education at Ludlow had been supervised by Lord Rivers, a man known to be an outstanding jouster and a great soldier, who had to wear what must have been an uncomfortable hair shirt yet remained mostly affable.

With King Henry locked away in the Tower, Edward solidified his power with a decisive battle at Tewkesbury. Margaret of Anjou had returned from France via Weymouth and Exmouth enroute to Tewkesbury. Bands of Yorkist soldiers had forced their way into Tewkesbury Abbey and ran riot through its sacred buildings. The Lancastrians were finally defeated by Edward and it was there that Henry and Margaret's only child Prince Edward met his end and his mother was captured.[135] This battle saw the end of the majority of the male bloodline within the Lancastrian house, hence Cecily's fortune at one year old (ancestor born Bonville). Allegedly, Henry VI was stabbed to death in the Tower of London as his body was found at the Tower in June 1471. Through battle and bloodshed, the Yorkist forces had managed to obtain and retain control. Edward IV was restored to the throne after the last battle of 1471 when his own son was five months old.

Edward IV was restored to the throne until his death in 1483

The Yorks went to Baynard's Castle for Mass and an overnight stay then Edward returned victoriously to London accompanied by his brothers

134 The History Jar: English History from 1066, 'Kirby Muxloe Castle and William, Lord Hastings'.
135 *Kings and Queens of the British Isles*, pp.106-107.

George, 1st Duke of Clarence, and Richard, Duke of Gloucester (eventually to be Richard III). Consort Elizabeth persuaded him to release Margaret of Anjou from the Tower, to be moved to Windsor Castle under house arrest until 8 July 1471. Edward kindly had her sent to Wallingford Castle near Ewelme, Oxfordshire, although impermanently.[136]

Being a possible heir and with Edward IV in power, Margaret Beaufort's boy was in danger.[137] His escape took him to Brittany, where he remained for 12 years. Henry Stafford died in October 1471, probably from wounds inflicted at Barnet. Margaret took legal measures to ensure her estates inherited from her father would belong to her son Henry whenever he returned. To further protect her son, she married Thomas Stanley, Edward IV's steward, which expanded the couple's fortunes. Margaret's relationship to Edward's Queen Consort and Princess Elizabeth Plantagenet blossomed. During the Wars of the Roses, they would have had feminine exchanges and much fear and worry in common. As key mothers, they were in communication concerning the possibility of their children Henry Tudor and Elizabeth Plantagenet marrying.

Edward IV was a generous and discriminating patron of the arts. He took a keen interest in the new invention of printing, financing the first book printed in England, *The Dictes and Sayenges of the Phylosophers*, translated into English by the Queen's eldest brother Anthony Woodville, Lord Rivers, and printed by William Caxton in 1477.[138]

In 1482, Margaret Beaufort's mother died. Edward IV agreed to confirm Henry Tudor's title to the lands Margaret had placed in trust and also to Henry's rights to share income from his maternal grandmother's estates, but only on his return to England. Dynastic unrest had mostly disappeared until Edward died suddenly on 9 April 1483, succeeded by his son now 12-year-old Edward V and his royal uncle, Richard his protector. Sir William Parr took part in the funeral of Edward IV in 1483, the year of his own death, and was urged by Lady FitzHugh to accept and follow the rule of Richard during the minority of the young King. Meanwhile, Henry Tudor returned with military support to England from Brittany in 1483 but his journey was delayed by bad weather and Richard overcame an attempted rebellion.

136 Alison Weir, *Lancaster and York: the Wars of the Roses*, p.419.

137 John Johnson Lewis, *Margaret Beaufort Biography*.

138 *Kings and Queens of the British Isles*, p.107.

Edward V – reigned 1483

Richard had chosen to wait until Edward was dead before accusing him of bigamy, prior to heir Edward V's coronation. It depends when Stillington told Richard about Edward's prior marriage. From being someone of little notice to the keeper of the Privy Seal, as well as Bishop of Bath and Wells under Edward IV when Edward's secret marriage to Elizabeth was about to become public knowledge and no known priest had been required for an irregular marriage but shrewd Elizabeth had taken the precaution of having her mother there as an additional witness, no first-hand testimonies survive. Fourteen years later, Stillington was put in the Tower as was Edward's brother George (Clarence). Had Stillington told Clarence about the pre-contract?[139] There is no evidence that Edward obtained a Papal Dispensation to regularise his marriage to Elizabeth Woodville Grey. Had the marriage remained irregular, the union itself would have been legal but children of the marriage would be barred from inheriting. Asking the pope for a dispensation perhaps meant Edward lying about his marital status, a very deceitful act. Likewise, Richard should have had the matter tried in an ecclesiastical court to be certain that his nephew had no claim to the throne, he could have been in the right. Historians tend to accept that Eleanor had definitely been a mistress of Edward.

Edward V was summoned to London from Ludlow. Hastings wrote to Richard informing him of Edward IV's death and warning of the danger of a Woodville coup. Council met in London where there were arguments between the Woodville faction and older nobles, including Hastings, concerning the coronation being too hasty. On 24 April 1483, Edward V and 2nd Lord Rivers set out for London with 2000 men. They found messengers on the road and agreed to meet Gloucester and Buckingham in Northampton. Sir Richard Grey (Edward V's half-brother) came from London to Northampton to find the new King gone. Lord Rivers was imprisoned and Sir Richard Grey arrested. Elizabeth Woodville went into sanctuary with her remaining children at Westminster Abbey. Morton gave the Great Seal to Elizabeth for safe-keeping. Hastings told Richard what Morton had done but said that Rivers and Grey would receive impartial justice. Morton was sacked as Lord

139 The History Jar: English History from 1066, 'Eleanor Butler – the holiest harlot or an unrecognised Queen'.

Chancellor but still kept his seat on the Council as a bishop: Richard now had control while Hastings possibly resented his power.

Richard wrote letters to Sir Richard Ratcliffe, Mayor of York, and the Earl of Northumberland stating that he believed the Woodvilles intended to murder him.[140] Anthony Woodville, 2nd Earl Rivers was beheaded at Pontefract in June 1483.[141] He bequeathed Scales' lands to his brother Edward, who used the Scales name unofficially; he was actually given Lordship of the Isle of Wight. The title Earl Rivers passed to the 3rd and last Earl Rivers, after whose death in 1491 the title became extinct. His will chose Thomas Grey, Marquess of Dorset, as his heir, to whom he left all his lands. He desired that he should sell as much underwood from the woods at Grafton as would buy a bell for the parish church to serve as a memorial to the last of the Woodvilles of Grafton. Dorset was son and heir of John Lord Ferrers of Groby, Elizabeth Woodville's first husband. Queen Elizabeth I was to be at Grafton in June and July 1575 where she held council meetings.

English turmoil returned but left only questionable evidence behind. Robert Stillington claimed that not only had a pre-contract to marriage with another woman existed, but that he had witnessed an exchange of vows. This would mean Edward was a bigamist and all his children with Elizabeth illegitimate. A *Titulus Regius* bastardised young King Edward V, who lost his crown as his uncle, Richard III, his father's brother (Duke of Gloucester), seized the throne.

Richard III – reigned 1483-1485

Subsequent to Edward IV's death, Hastings had sent a message to Richard in Middleham to say that the Woodvilles should wait until Richard arrived in London. Two days later, Richard was proclaimed King. When Richard took the throne, Parr was not impressed, detesting the usurpation. Dominic Mancini was in London for a short period from circa 1482 until shortly before Richard's coronation on 6 July 1483. Mancini wrote a small book the title of which translates as *The Usurpation of Richard III.* His account survives in a unique 16th century copy discovered by C.A.J. Armstrong, who edited it in 1969.[142]

---

140 The History Jar: English History from 1066, 'Kirby Muxloe Castle and William, Lord Hastings'.

141 BHO, 'Grafton Regis'. Fn. 121 *Complete Peerage*, xi. 22-24. Fn. 151 Acts of P.C. 1511-1515, 400-402; ibid. 1575-1577, 3-4.

142 The History of England, Cerdic, *Dominic Mancini*. Dominic Mancini, *The Usurpation of Richard III,* (n.d.) translation (2016). From unique 16th century copy ed. C.A.J. Armstrong (1969). *https://thehistoryofengland.co.uk/resource/dominic.mancini/* [accessed 27 April 2020].

There was no evidence that Rivers fought Richard of Gloucester, although the royal escort men had outnumbered his and Edward V was already safely elsewhere. They had not hurried from Ludlow and may have been unaware of what was happening in London. When Rivers got there, his soldiers might have seemed confrontational. Suspicion already surrounded the Woodvilles because they had not notified Richard of Edward IV's death. This caused bad feeling but protecting the two Princes was surely understandable as Rivers was keeping his own nephew safe.

Some historians believe that Margaret Beaufort was part of a failed attempt to rescue Elizabeth's sons.[143] Maybe Hastings had foreseen that Richard planned to usurp the throne. Mancini thought that Hastings needed to be killed in order for Richard to claim the crown. On 13 June 1485, Hastings was accused of plotting and treason, he was immediately beheaded in the courtyard of the Tower of London after his confession was heard by a cleric: this was another execution without trial – a murder. Also, Lords Stanley and Morton were imprisoned. Three days later, Richard went into the Tower to visit the young Princes, who were under his protection, knowing that Edward IV's legal will identified him as regent. With Edward V in the Tower and his younger brother Richard Plantagenet alongside, both died in suspicious circumstances, Richard III was blamed.

The Croyland Chronicle reported that Richard invented the story of Edward's prior marriage to justify his usurpation of the throne.[144] No longer Queen Consort, Elizabeth was treated badly by Richard III; she lost her dower rights when her marriage to Edward IV was declared invalid.[145] Richard's parliament in 1484 declared that Jacquetta had used witchcraft to procure her daughter's marriage to Edward.[146]

Sir William Parr did not attend Richard III's coronation but returned north despite being given a place as canopy bearer. This was even though Lady Parr and his mother were two of seven noble ladies appointed to serve

---

143 John Johnson Lewis, *Margaret Beaufort Biography.*

144 *Ingulph's Chronicle of the Abbey of Croyland:* with the Continuations by Peter of Blois and Anonymous Writers. Ingulf Peter (of Blois) H.G. Bohn (1 January 1854), [free e-book from] *https://play.google.com/store/books/details?id=KIIOAAAAQAAJ&rdid=book-KIIOAAAAQAAJ&rdot=1*

145 John Johnson Lewis, *Margaret Beaufort Biography.*

146 History Extra, the official website for *BBC History Magazine*... '8 things you (probably) didn't know about the Woodvilles'. *https://www.historyextra.com/* [accessed 5 June 2020].

Queen Consort Anne. Henry VIII's wife, Catherine Parr, was of the same Parr family.[147] Hastings' titles, estates and wealth were soon rightfully restored to their heirs by Richard III.[148] Charley Marsteller, a lineal descendant of Hastings, certainly concluded that Richard was a murderer but does this saga's writer agree? Not in regard to the fate of the Princes in the Tower because there seems to be insufficient evidence. *The Croyland Chronicle* reported very little about the Princes in the Tower, but any reporting would have been speculative and prejudiced anyway. Although it was usually seen as an authoritative, almost contemporary, chronicle, it was written after the Battle of Bosworth by an eye witness, probably a senior civil servant.[149]

22 August 1485, Battle of Bosworth Field, House of Tudor Victory

Henry Tudor was determined both to take the crown from Richard and marry Elizabeth of York. Richard had ordered Parliament to take control of Margaret Beaufort's property in favour of her husband; all the trusts protecting their son young Henry's inheritance were reversed. In Stanley's custody she fared well and remained in communication with Henry, who sailed again in 1485, this time landing in Wales. Stanley deserted Richard's side to support Henry Tudor. Richard III was killed.

In September 2012 a skeleton was found beneath a city council car park in central Leicester, beyond reasonable doubt it was discovered to be the remains of Richard III, who would have been 32 years old when he died. Evidence of scoliosis was revealed in his body and it was accepted that he would have been buried there hastily in 1485 beneath the church of Greyfriars, which had been demolished during the Reformation.[150]

16 June 1487, Battle of Stoke-by-Newark[151 152]

This battle was another victory for Henry Tudor, finally overcoming the Plantagenet dynasty and bringing the House of Tudor to England.

147 Linda Porter, *Katherine, The Queen* (2010).

148 The History Jar: English History from 1066, 'Kirby Muxloe Castle and William, Lord Hastings'.

149 The History of England, Cerdic, 'The Fate of the Princes – Evidence' (2017). *https://thehistoryofengland.co.uk/resource/the-fate-of-the-princes-evidence/* [accessed 27 April 2020].

150 BBC, 'Richard III dig: DNA confirms bones are king's', *BBC News* (4 February 2013). *https://www.bbc.co.uk/news/uk-england-leicestershire-21063882* [accessed 5 June 2020].

151 The Finer Times, 'Wars of the Roses'

152 Bruce Webster, *The Wars of the Roses*.

Henry VII – reigned 1485-1509

Henry VII declared himself King and was crowned by right of battle rather than by Lancastrian heritage or by being the last claimant to the throne. He dated the start of his reign to the day before the battle, which allowed him to be the one who charged Richard's soldiers with treason and seized their properties and titles. The union between Henry and Elizabeth, Tudor and York, ended the Wars of the Roses.[153] That is a very significant fact and would be worthy until one remembers how horrific and ignorant those times really were in England then. The whole bloody story was significant to royalty and nobles but less so to lower classes. Of course, the Tudor rose is a combination of red and white, a moderate choice for such an extremist nation. The magnates had been brilliant opportunists when it came to changing sides.

Lords paid congregations to pray for them. John VI de Sutton, 20th Dudley Baron (born 1400/1401) was buried at Dudley Priory in 1487. He desired spending £20 on a tomb, plus other costs to include twenty marks in money to be disposed in alms on that day and on the morrow to poor people to pray for his soul and that of his wife Elizabeth (m. 1421/2, died 1478) and all friends. Also he desired that:

> "one thousand masses to be said for me as soon as possible after my burial, which masses to cost £16.13s.4d."[154]

He reached a great age, had a varied life and proved himself to be a respected diplomat. Constable of the Tower in 1473, he was described as the greatest of the barons of Dudley.

Richard III's Queen was Anne Neville, daughter of 'The Kingmaker' Richard Neville, Earl of Warwick and Salisbury (d. 1471). Elizabeth Grey (circa 1480-1525) 6th Baroness Lisle, descendant of Warwick and Shrewsbury, married Edmund Dudley (1462-1510) her first husband. Their son would be John Dudley, 1st Duke of Northumberland, 1st Earl of Warwick, Dudley 23rd Baron and Viscount Lisle.

---

153 John Johnson Lewis, *Margaret Beaufort Biography.*

154 John Hemingway, *An Illustrated Chronicle of the Cluniac Priory of St. James*, p.46.

Chapter 4

Reforming Tudors?

IT SEEMS best to begin with the backdrop of the royal Tudor dynasty before moving to understand what the 21st-25th Dudley Barons were experiencing. Afterwards the tree introduces a new branch, another direct family line crossing the horizon. The mystery of how the Danish royal family joined this saga is tantalising but explained, as far as possible, towards the end of Elizabethan times when Stuart rule was nigh.

Henry VII – reigned 1485-1509

Henry VII appointed John Morton to be Lord Chancellor of England in 1487. In this capacity, Morton restored the royal estate depleted by King Edward IV. By the end of Henry's reign, his own frugality and Morton's tax policy as carried out by Lord Edmund Dudley (b.1462) and Richard Empson had replenished the treasury. Morton made a rule that no-one could be exempt from taxes, this was known as 'Morton's Fork'. Crowther's opinion was that Edmund Dudley (b.1462) along with Sir Richard Empson were Henry VII's hatchet men:

> "Edmund (b.1462) specialised in the prerogative rights of the King, which qualified him very well for Henry VII's purposes. He was elected to Parliament in 1491-2 and again in 1495 as knight of the shire for Sussex. In 1504 Henry VII appointed him Speaker of the Commons. From 1504 he received £66 as a councillor of the King and was also part of the council learned in law. By July 1506, he was president of the King's

council, the first layman to hold the position. Evidently Edmund's rise to power was rapid. He maintained meticulous accounts; his role was to manage the King's use of a range of ways to exploit his greater subjects. [Edmund] sold offices, wardships and licences to marry the widows of tenants-in-chief, pardons for treason, sedition, murder, riot, retaining and other offences. In less than four years, he collected £219,316 in cash and bonds [securing] future payments, [all viciously enforcing] the King's rights."[155]

The Great Chronicle of London recorded:

> "the chief lords of England were glad to be in his favour, and were eager to go to him for many urgent causes."

He knew the ways of London, uncovered customs fraud and coinage offences, raised customs rates and forced the King's candidates for civic office on the citizens. For the King's confirmation of London's liberties, he extracted £3,333. Further reporting from *The Great Chronicle of London* lamented:

> "whosoever had the sword borne before him, Dudley was mayor, and what his pleasure was, was done."

Consequently, this Edmund attracted enemies. At Paul's Cross and elsewhere, preachers strongly railed against his profit-making for himself and the crown. By 1509, Dudley had amassed £550 per year gross from landed estates in 16 counties plus £5,000 or more in goods.

As for Empson, Crowther wrote:

> "Empson relentlessly strove to increase the King's revenue as Chancellor. He raised rents, cancelled rebates, ran surveys and audits and investigated feudal dues. As part of the Council Learned he pursued the King's debtors and his techniques were not pretty. He dug out approvers, third parties

155 David Crowther, *Henry VII's Hatchet Men: Empson and Dudley*. The History of England; great history podcasts from the shed. *https://thehistoryofengland.co.uk/resource/henry-viis-hatchet-men-empson-and-dudley/* [accessed 18 June 2020]. *The Great Chronicle of London*. (Edmund Dudley), *The Tree of Commonwealth* (1509).

> who would bring prosecutions against individuals; he imprisoned people to force them to settle fines, he issued official summons by privy seal but victims then found themselves in front of Empson at his own London manor of St. Brides. He raised money also by pardons, countersigned by the King, uncovering forfeitures on outlawry: exploiting wards. Where he found wrong doing, the result was usually a fine to the King."

Henry VII fully trusted Empson, even allowing him to execute his will. Empson and Dudley were both fall guys for Henry. On 24 April 1509, three days after Henry VII's death, Empson was arrested for treason and accused of protecting himself with armed men as and when Henry was dying. Charged at Northampton, he was convicted and sentenced to death, he was attained in the Parliament of January-February 1510.

Dudley had been tried in London in 1509, accused of planning to hold, guide and govern the King and his council. Having probably assembled a force of men, it was a time of political uncertainty, he was convicted for treason. However, it was unlikely he intended a *coup d'etat*. In the Tower and feeling harshly treated, Edmund composed a petition and sent it to Richard Foxe and Thomas Lovell, making it clear that Henry was responsible for policy. Also, he took time to compose a treatise on government and society entitled *The Tree of Commonwealth*.[156] Both Empson and Dudley were beheaded on Tower Hill on the 17 August. Crowther concluded that they were reputed to be hatchet men for Henry and that they were characterised by Polydore Vergil and others as extortioners. Dudley had confessed a long list of individuals he had wronged. Nevertheless, everything the two men did was sanctioned and encouraged by Henry VII: they were his loyal and faithful servants.

Henry VIII – reigned 1509-1547

Henry VIII's reign passed through a dynamic period for English society. Remnants of the feudal system still existed alongside a growth of professional and commercial bourgeoisie while traditional nobles, peers and the greater gentry still represented a social elite with political and economic clout.[157]

---

156 Edmund Dudley (b. 1462), *The Tree of Commonwealth* (circa 1509).

157 *The Tudors: England 1485-1603, A-Level and AS* Component 1, ed. Michael Tillbrook (Oxford, 2015), illus. (Oxford AQA history, series ed. Sally Waller).

John A. Parke was one of about 100 named richest citizens in Dudley required to pay a lay subsidy of 5s tax. Less wealthy citizens paid only 4d. This was required in connection with Henry VIII's wish to rid his kingdom of the Catholic Church. He began with easy targets that included Dudley Priory. If paid, the levy would have raised £416s 8d. Henry had removed the name of the Pope in service books but some churchwardens did not scratch the name out, they merely lined it through lightly. Protestantism was not fully achieved by Henry VIII.

There were deserving and undeserving poor: the former were entitled to receive limited help whereas Tudors now thought the latter should be punished. Deserving people were mostly disabled, widowed or old and were accepted as being unable to work. The undeserving tended to be vagabonds, wandering from place to place, homeless and unemployed. Such souls might have been a threat to law and order but would be seen as suffering from mental disorders, sadness or other genuine kinds of problems. Before the Reformation, the church had the main responsibility for giving poor relief. Thomas Wolsey, Henry's chief minister, was at the summit of his prestige and power by 1518. Needing a united Christian front, the Pope appointed him as Papal Legate for England; the role meant Wolsey represented the Pope and had control over the English church, raising his status above that of the Archbishop of Canterbury.

Historian Alan Dyer wrote that economic difficulties were apparent over much of the Midlands in the 16th century, but there were few signs of unusual wealth in this area in the late middle-ages. South Staffordshire's iron and coal industries created several new towns. As it was, Staffordshire was a poor and economically marginal county before the 18th century and contained no dominant towns. The Black Country, in the extreme south of Staffordshire, provided no unifying centre and was undistinguishable then. Birmingham was only a 'middling market town' in the 1560s like scores of others.[158]

King Henry VIII's final act of dissolution took place in 1539. Idolatry, stained glass windows, wall paintings, sculptures and bell ringing were outlawed. Nevertheless, he began the English Reformation moderately compared with later monarchs. He craved Catholicism without the Pope.

---

158 Alan Dyer, 'Midlands' in *The Cambridge Urban History of Britain 1540-1840*, ed. Peter Clark (Cambridge, 2000), vol. II, pp.93-110.

In response to the papal claim to exercise power even in temporal matters, lawyers used *'rex in regno suo est imperator'*, meaning that without domination the Pope had no authority to legislate for the Kingdom, no dominium over the King's subjects. The theory of 'imperial' monarchy was disseminated by civil lawyers on behalf of the French monarch against the Pope. Henry VIII and Francis I claimed to be emperors in their kingdoms but only Henry broke with Rome, seeing himself as God's vicar on earth whose catchment encompassed church and state. His redefinition of 'empire' was Caesar-papalist in the view of political historian John Guy.[159] Henry VIII claimed that the Pope was no better than any human legislator who had exceeded his authority and was inferior to the General Council, which could depose him.

During Henry VIII's reign, Nicolaus Copernicus (b.1473) had dared to claim that the earth was not the centre of the Universe and published his work for consideration in 1543. Renaissance ideas were beginning to flourish amongst elite groups within English society. Henry had felt ready to encourage thinkers like Desiderius Erasmus and Thomas More.[160] He commissioned the Florentine sculptor, Pietro Torrigiano, to produce in Renaissance classical style the tombs of his parents, Henry VII and Elizabeth of York, and of his grandmother Lady Margaret Beaufort, situated in the Lady Chapel of Westminster.

Edward VI – reigned 1547-1553

England was struck by economic problems as well as by conflicts with France and Scotland. Edward VI's uncle, the Earl of Hertford, disbanded Henry VIII's Council of Regents and proclaimed himself Lord Protector of his nephew. The King agreed to raise Hertford to Duke of Somerset, by which name he is best remembered. He was a radical Protestant, imposing on the church the 1549 *Act of Uniformity* and Cranmer's *Book of Common Prayer* with new liturgy in English; emphasising prayer, praise and study; aiming to simplify the Roman Catholic missal.[161] [162] Somerset's measures against land enclosures infuriated Parliament too.

---

159 Adams, Simon and P. Collinson, eds., 'Britain Europe and the World' in *Short History of the British Isles: The Sixteenth Century* (Oxford, 2002). See also contribution by John Guy (Oxford, 2001).

160 *The Tudors*, p.115-117.

161 Parliament, *Act of Uniformity* (1549).

162 Thomas Cranmer, *Books of Common Prayer*, first issued March 1549, revised 1552, modified 1559 and mandatory under Elizabeth I.

Under King Edward VI, there had been a plan, never implemented, to divide the bishopric of Durham and to appropriate much of its wealth to the Crown.[163] During earlier Tudor times, Durham and Canterbury were important cities as saints' cults brought many pilgrims.

Thomas Wall, the early farmer-parson of Dudley died in 1551. From his will dated July 1550 we know that he had meagre household possessions and owed 6s 5d to creditors, mostly Dudley people. The value of his estate was £13 1s 1d. Dudley vicars enjoyed extensive glebe lands. St. Thomas's Parish was large and included distant places like Dudley Wood, Netherton, New Park, Kingswinford and Sedgley. His mare and colt had the highest value (45 shillings). Dudley houses had little furniture, the vicarage no exception. Thomas owned a spinning wheel and two pairs of "cardes" for use. He was neither much better off nor much worse off than his parishioners. Two fellow clergy had loaned him money: Jeremy Skett 11s 8d and Richard Wilkes £1 0s 0d. He must have witnessed and experienced problems brought about by the Reformation, the dissolution of the Priory and both his churches, to say nothing of having to introduce new forms of service to bewildered congregations. His successor was Thomas Bekensall, instituted on 13 August 1551. The prior and the convent were no longer responsible for the choice of Dudley's vicar and so Sir John Dudley chose the next parson from further afield.[164] By 1576 the gentry shared ideals within their Shyre of Worcester: of antiquity, continuity, piety, charity and unity, which ignored truths of inequalities like social mobility and land redistribution. Newcomers to the county were Lord Coventry, the Earl of Shrewsbury, Lord Windsor, Walter Devereux and Sir Robert Berkeley.

Mary I – reigned 1553-1558

During her reign, Mary brought back Latin Mass, rituals and some forms of monasticism. Wyatt's Rebellion of 1554 had partly been sparked by popular suspicion concerning the Catholic marriage between Mary and Philip II of Spain and the almost 'dare not be spoken' prospect of a Catholic reign. The crown's forces held London Bridge from rebels trying to advance across the Thames from the Southwark bank of the river on 3 February. This was a critical

163 *The Tudors,* pp.38, 136.

164 Dudley Archives. (Information on Dudley vicars).

turning point and there were Protestant victims.[165] Mary was convinced that Elizabeth had been aware of the rebellion, therefore she had her arrested on Palm Sunday 18 March 1554. Elizabeth was confined to the Tower and not released until 19 May 1554. Mary's poor health caused her own death on 17 November 1558.

Elizabeth I – reigned 1558-1603

Elizabeth I's injunctions were meant to be controlling, her religious settlement was merely an act of State, defining the relationship between crown and church. It comprised *The Act of Supremacy*, *Act of Uniformity*, plus a set of royal injunctions and a single *Book of Common Prayer*, all 1559.[166] [167] [168] Her subjects varied in how they interpreted religious settlement. Many of her close advisers thought it represented a fresh spiritual renewal: the establishment of a true Church of England, which would turn England into God's nation elect.

Under Elizabeth I, churchwardens recorded those who failed to turn up to church services. Such persons had to contribute to the poor man's box, for example an amount of twelve pence was required at the time unless they had good reasons for absences. Much policing was done by churchwardens, bailiffs, and reeves. Anyone in breach of ecclesiastical law, or living immorally, was reported to the local archdeaconry court by parish churchwardens.

Hoping to regain Calais, Elizabeth attempted to pressurise the French monarchy while it was in a weak state. The Queen paid a Huguenot army, led by the Prince of Conde, to fight on the Protestant side. Both sides lost their leaders and the Duke of Guise, a Catholic, was assassinated. England signed the subsequent Treaty of Troyes in 1564, Calais could not be regained and it was an unfavourable settlement. This caused Elizabeth to be cautious about supporting Protestant causes on the European continent.

Benthem stressed the need for use of the *Book of Common Prayer* in 1565.[169] He wanted altars to be replaced by tables, churches to discard idols and superstitious monuments. Holy water had to go as did hand bells

---

165 *The Tudors*, pp.160-161.

166 Parliament, *Act of Supremacy* (1559).

167 Parliament, *Act of Uniformity* (1559).

168 *Book of Common Prayer* (1559).

169 *Book of Common Prayer.*

and sepulchres and he told clergy to practise clear recitation and to tighten discipline. Many of the local gentry and nobility were strong Catholics and allowed chaplains and priests to take Mass in their houses. Some eventually provided priest holes as hiding spaces. Recusancy was the refusal to conform to the Elizabethan Anglican Settlement despite resulting in fines, imprisonment, even death. An early martyr was Robert Sutton, son of a Burton carpenter, who was caught saying Mass inside Stafford County Gaol for which crime he was executed.

Every region acquired a 'survey' of its past, a national trend. Erdeswicke's *Survey of Staffordshire* was circulated in manuscript form.[170] Richard Grafton's *Chronicle at Large* of 1568 for instance and Raphael Hollinshed's *Chronicles* of 1577, which Shakespeare later applied to his history plays.[171] [172]

By absolving Catholic subjects in 1570 from respecting her as their sovereign, Elizabeth responded to this excommunication by allowing disobedience while she and her Council tightened treason law in acts of frightening retaliation. Protestants were branded as loyalists, Catholics as traitors.[173] The Dudley Sutton barons appear to have been loyalists.

Townspeople became proud of possessing their own courts and economic/social arrangements. People found independence and citizenship. Ideas were disseminated through books and pamphlets, schools were centred in towns; Philip Sidney (related to the Dudleys) was educated at Shrewsbury School. People flocked to church on Sundays and Saints' days. The Queen tended to emphasise liturgy whereas clergy found preaching important and singers loved the music. Around 1578, trades and professions were busy in town markets while fairs and festivals also thrived. However, the lord of the manor could be wary of the rising status of townsfolk. Elizabethan clothes symbolised village elites who were able to afford such attire. Bourgeoisie, known as 'middling sorts', increased in number from the time of Henry's reign but remained a social step down from rich merchants and town craftsmen. There were cultural differences between sociable town dwellers and more rustic Christians.

---

170 Erdeswicke's *Survey of Staffordshire* (circulated in manuscript form).

171 Richard Grafton, *Chronicles at Large* (1568).

172 Raphael Holinshed, *Chronicles* (1577).

173 *The Tudors*, pp.197-198.

Sutton Dudley Barons and their families

Edward, Sutton 2nd, Dudley 21st Baron (c.1465-1532)

Direct ancestor Dudley 21st Baron was the son of Edmund Sutton (1425-1485) and so grandson of John de Sutton 1st, Dudley 20th Baron (1400-1487), whose wives were Elizabeth Berkeley and Catherine Clivedon. This saga is of the Berkeley line.

Edward was invited to Parliament twice around the turn of the century, in 1497 and 1504. One of Edward's wards was John, son of John Grey, Lord of Powis. Under Henry VII's *Statute of Liveries*, he had to pay £1,000 plus £50 per year to the crown for Grey's property. His cousin, Edmund Dudley (b.1462) was responsible for this demand.[174] [175] Further debts were exploited from the 21st Baron in 1508. Henry VIII came to the throne the following year. Edward may have borrowed money from John Barel to cover his own expenses at the coronation.

Tothill Street, near the west front of Westminster Abbey, is the most ancient street in the vicinity, it was inhabited by noblemen as well as "the flower of the gentry." The Bishop of Chester resided there in 1488, Lord Dudley began renting a house in Tothill from St. Mary's fraternity in 1522. London perhaps seemed convenient and inviting to the 21st Baron, when the house became the Suttons' home near Parliament.[176] Sir Andrew Dudley lived and died there. Lord Grey of Wilton was nearby in a place later known as Strutton Ground. Regional gentry's marriage patterns in England provided evidence that the measure to which local elites were exposed to influences from London was not confined to a minority of eminent families.[177]

The risk of disease was high in greater London. Cecily Grey of Groby, 7th Baroness of Harington (born Bonville), died of sweating sickness in 1529. By Elizabeth's reign, there were houses on both sides of Tothill Street. On the north side they had large gardens that reached to St. James' Park, south

---

174 Public Records Office, *Inquisitions Post Mortem* (formerly known as escheal – probate). (London, 2019). *https://publicrecordsearch.co.uk/england* [accessed 18 June 2020].

175 Parliament, *Statute of Liveries.*

176 John Hemingway, *An Illustrated Chronicle of the Castle and Barony of Dudley 1070-1757*, (Dudley, 2006), pp.70-73, 105, maps, b & w. and col. Illus. All Rights Reserved. Illus. of The Carew ring found in excavation in 1980s, DUCAP.

177 Ian Warren, 'London's impact on the English Gentry: The case of Worcestershire, c. 1580-1680' in *Midland History*, 33(2) (2008), 156-178.

side gardens were extensive too, down as far as Orchard Street. Later in this saga, Elwell direct ancestors are linked with the name Carew, which might be relevant as Carew House stood near the Gate House on Strutton Ground, where Sir George Carew died in 1612.[178]

John (Henry) Sutton, Dudley 22nd Dudley Baron (c.1494-1553)

The 22nd Dudley Baron was unfortunately known in later life as Lord Quondam, meaning 'Lord Wants' due to the destitution that befell him. State papers showed that John's estates were sold and divided between himself, the Earl of Shrewsbury and others. Poor Cecily, his wife, was born Grey of Dorset, Dudley 24th's mother, 16th generation ancestor in this saga and descendant of Elizabeth Woodville with Grey line. She wrote to Thomas Cromwell in February 1537 complaining of the poverty in which she and her husband were forced to live. She claimed that she only had £20 a year to live on for herself, her daughter and two others and had to rely on Agnes Oulton, the prioress of Nuneaton for meat and drink. She was apparently living at the priory at that time.[179]

This impoverishment was to have a detrimental effect on the lives of the 24th and 25th Dudley barons. Between the years 1496-1553, Himley belonged to the Earl of Shrewsbury not the Dudleys, but Dodonis Sutton Dudley (Dud, 1599-1684) was familiar with Himley as it was only four miles from Dudley Castle. Both 24th and 25th barons had multiple expenses other than being extravagant when it came to home and garden splendours.

John Dudley, 1st Duke of Northumberland, 23rd Dudley Baron (1501-1553)

The barons Sutton Dudley comprised the senior line of the family but they were undistinguished even in Staffordshire compared with the junior branch, which were prominent through the behaviour of John Dudley, Duke of Northumberland (Earl of Warwick). A cousin from the junior side, he encouraged Somerset's Protestant reforms because he foresaw opportunities coming his way from ensuing wealth. Greed, personal power and loyalty to

178 BHO, 'Westminster: Tothill Fields and Neighbourhood in Old and New London', Edward Walford (London, 1878), Vol. 4, pp.14-26. *http://www.british-history.ac.uk/old-new-london/vol4/pp14-26* [accessed 12 June 2020].

179 *Tudorplace*, 'Cecily Grey', Tudorplace.com *http://www.tudorplace.com* [accessed 26 June 2020].

his monarch drove his extremist administration to pass repressive laws.[180] [181] His Parliamentary opposition resulted in Somerset's downfall and subsequent execution in 1552.

Northumberland was cheeky enough to match his son, Guildford Dudley, with Lady Jane Grey (1537-1554) a devout Protestant girl, who was married off unwillingly on 21 May 1553. With young King Edward VI unwell, the Duke convinced his Protestant monarch that the crown must not go to Catholic Mary. Very ill, the King died on 6 July 1553 by which time he had subtly changed the wording of *The Devyse* concerning succession to his throne, particularly Jane's intentions, from "L. Janes heires masles" to "LJan and her heires masles."[182] [183] [184] Jane was a great-niece of Henry VIII through his youngest sister Mary Rose. Also, she was a direct descendant of Elizabeth Woodville and John Grey of Groby. Jane's parents were Henry Grey (created Duke of Suffolk in 1551, previously 3rd Marquess of Dorset) and Frances (born Brandon).

Lady Jane Grey, 'Nine day Queen' 1553

So Northumberland schemed to place his quiet new daughter-in-law on the English throne. She was proclaimed Queen on 10 July 1553 but her claim was weak and she lacked backing. On hearing of Northumberland's intentions, Mary had gathered Catholic supporters. Meanwhile, Northumberland summoned troops and a naval squadron off Great Yarmouth to curb any plan Mary might have to sail. This tactic failed because he already had a reputation for cruelty in Norfolk.[185] Consequently, the county claimed allegiance to Mary. Loyalty spread and the Privy Council declared Mary I Queen on 19 July 1553 and so Henry VIII's eldest daughter, Roman Catholic Mary Tudor, took the throne from Jane, who was imprisoned in the Tower of London.

---

180 *The Tudors*, p.135.

181 Britain Express: Passionate about British History, 'Lady Jane Grey', ed. David Ross, illus. *https://www.britainexpress.com/History/tudor/grey.htm* [accessed 7 June 2020].

182 Stephen Alford, *Kingship and Politics in the Reign of Edward VI* (Cambridge, 2002), pp.171-172. Edward VI, *My devise for the succession.*

183 Britain Express: Passionate about British History, 'Lady Jane Grey'.

184 Ian Mortimer, *The Time Traveller guide to Elizabethan England* (London, 2013), illus. Fn. 71 Michael Bennett, 'Edward III's Entail and the Succession of the crown, 1376-1471', Michael Bennett (1998) *EHR*, 113, pp.580-609 (at p.606).

185 *The Tudors*, p.146.

As monarch, Mary I posed a threat to the Reformation and the wealth it brought. Her overthrow of Northumberland and Edward's *Devyse* had restored Henry VIII's will and, under the *Succession Act* of 1544, the legal mechanism for determining the succession.[186] [187] Mary would be succeeded by her half-sister Elizabeth should she die childless, despite their religious differences. Lady Catherine Grey (1540-1568) was Jane Grey's sister and therefore also grand-daughter of Henry VIII's sister Mary Rose. According to the terms of Henry VIII's will this made her Elizabeth's heir presumptive. This had seemed alright to him as she was a Protestant prospect. However, a scandal arose concerning her secret marriage to the Earl of Hertford, the couple were imprisoned in the Tower by Elizabeth I and the marriage was annulled in 1562.

Jane's father had joined the ill-fated Wyatt revolt and tried to involve the Midlands. Soon he was captured, which made Mary realise what a risk rebellion was as long as Jane lived. Consequently, she signed Jane's death warrant on 7 February 1554. Guildford Dudley was imprisoned in the Beauchamp Tower while Jane was put into the house of the gaoler on Tower Green. Although initially spared, 17-year-old Jane, the nine-day Queen soon met her fate. The couple were brought to trial for treason on 13 November and subsequently both were executed on 12 February 1554. *The Execution of Lady Jane Grey in the Tower of London* by Paul Delaroche is a sadly moving painting, especially as Mary had initially spared her. Alas, even worse, Mary pursued a policy to burn over 300 of Edward VI's Protestant activists for heresy, including Thomas Cranmer, whose own relationship with Northumberland had been disagreeable.[188]

Northumberland's Execution, Tower Hill, 22 August 1553

Northumberland was tried on 18 August in Westminster Hall for his part in promoting Jane as Queen and Mary I ordered his execution, having listened to his enemies on the Council reminding her how dangerous a man he was. A pamphlet appeared beforehand, calling him, "the great devil Dudley."[189] There again, some who knew him spoke well of his charm, intelligence and

---

186 Parliament, *Act of Succession* (1554).

187 *The Tudors*, pp.79, 129, 148.

188 Britain Express: Passionate about British History, 'Lady Jane Grey'. – Paul Delaroche, 'The Execution of Lady Jane Grey in the Tower of London'.

189 Stephen Alford, *Kingship and Politics in the Reign of Edward VI*, p.7. Edward VI, *My devise for the succession.*

dignity. He had been a crown servant perhaps capable of loyalty to whichever monarch reigned. In promoting Jane, he told his accomplices:[190]

> "This virtuous lady... by... our enticement is rather of force placed therein than by her own seeking and request."

Before death befell, he returned to Catholicism, saying,[191]

> "...beware of seditious preachers and teachers of new doctrine."

Dudley family ancestors were the de Somerys: Roger de Somery's widow, Agnes, inherited Prestwood Farm, Kinver, described as half a carucate with some meadow. After the death of John de Somery in 1322, the land had continued to be the property of Dudley Castle owners for a very long time until it was attainted for Northumberland's attempt at stopping Mary's accession. In 1554 Mary granted the land to Edward Hastings (Hastynges), who had then sold it to Sir John Lyttleton (1520-1590). The Dudley Estates were reverted to the Sutton line by Mary I as they too had been forfeited to the crown by the attainder of Edward Sutton Dudley's cousin Northumberland.

Sir Philip Sidney's opinion

The two most influential prose writers were Sir Philip Sidney and Edmund Spenser. Although political outsiders, quite capable of criticising Elizabeth, both mixed at court. Sidney adapted classical forms to modernise the English language and revived the sonnet in English poetry, by so doing he was a precursor of Shakespeare.[192] A discourse from Sidney provides contemporary evidence of noble eloquence and manners:

> "Now to the Dudleys... when he hath poured out all his flood of scolding eloquence, he saith they are no gentlemen, affirming that the

190 Eric Ives, *Lady Jane Grey: A Tudor Mystery* (2009), p.216.

191 W.K. Jordan and M.R. Gleason, *The Saying of John Late Duke of Northumberland upon the Scaffold 1553* (Harvard Library, 1975), pp.45-47.

192 Philip Sidney, 'A Discourse in Defence of the Earl of Leicester', *The Miscellaneous Works of Sir Philip Sidney, Knt* (1584). William Gray, ed., (Boston: T.O.H.P. Burnham, 1860), pp.305-323. (Luminarium editions, created in HTML by Anniina Jokinen of Luminarium, May 2007. The text was unaltered).

> then Duke of Northumberland was not born so... I should have studied with myself of points of false invections, which a poisonous tongue could have spit out against that duke... but this fellow doth like him. I am a Dudley in blood, that duke's daughter's son... I am by my father's side, of ancient, and always well-esteemed and well-matched gentry, yet I do acknowledge that my chiefest honour is to be a Dudley... this fellow of invincible shamelessness, would ever have called so palpable a matter in question. The house of Grey is well known... for number of great houses sprung of it, to be matched by none. The house of Berkeley... descended lineally from a king of Denmark, affirmed to be but hath ever been one of the best houses in England... England can boast of no nobler... their arms and name, as in old time they used in England and do daily in Spain, France and Italy... this house therefore of Dudley, which in despite of all shamelessness he so doth deprave, is this day a peer... a lord of the Parliament and so a companion, both in marriage, Parliament and trial, to the greatest duke that England can bear. In Harry the Fifth's time, the Lord Dudley was his Lord Steward, and did that pitiful office in bringing home, as the chief mourner, his victorious [master's] dead body; as who goes to Westminster in the church may see... yet did he but receive his nobility from his ancestors, who had been lords of that very seignory of Dudley Castle... even from King Richard the First's time; at which time Sir Richard Sutton married the daughter and heir of the Lord Dudley; since which time all descended of him, as divers[e] branches there be, left the name of Sutton, and have all been called Dudleys, which is now four hundred years since and both those houses of Sutton and Dudley, having been before that time of great nobility... that one of Saxon blood, as Sutton's name testifieth he was, should match with such an inheritrix as Dudley was... in England none, but the house of Stafford hath the like."

And:

> "...But hard it were, if every goose quill could any way blot the honour of an Earl of Leicester, written in the hearts of so many men through Europe... there is only such a nameless and shameless opposer... But to thee, I say, thou therin liest in thy throat; which I will be ready to

> justify upon thee, in any place of Europe, where thou wilt assign me a free place of coming, as within three months of the publishing hereof, I may understand thy mind... And this which I write I would send to thine own hands, if I knew thee; but I trust it cannot be intended, that he should be ignorant of this printed in London, which knows the very whisperings of the privy-chamber. I will make dainty of no baseness in thee, that art indeed the writer of this book. And, from the date of this writing, imprinted and published, I will three months expect thine answer."

How eloquent are Sidney's words, frankness slipping from his quill. Good manners prevailed amongst nobles yet this shows how polite language could be delivered with skilled insult. Pride in his noble family, even extending to Leicester's father, the executed Northumberland (Warwick before his promotion in 1551), and protecting Sidney's devotion to the required Protestantism was very important as such considerations constantly occupied Tudors. Sidney was quick to think he was opposing a man and one of Catholic faith. He defended the Earl of Leicester's pedigree as being high and suitable enough to match Elizabeth I, although the Queen did not listen to those advising her about marriage. Leicester and Sir Robert Cecil disagreed over a suitable husband for Elizabeth but co-operated over other issues.[193] The Queen was adamant about choosing her own husband or none. Whoever wrote the book Sidney referred to was a meddler, there again in his own turn of outrageous phrases, so was he. The date of Sidney's discourse is not disclosed, it came from a subsequent collection dated 1584.

In the role of Dudley Council Archaeological Officer in the 1980s, John Hemingway collected precise historical information when excavating Dudley Castle. Detailed facts can be found in his publications, including coverage of the Duke of Northumberland's life and character. Genealogical charts can be found in *An Illustrated Chronicle of the Castle and Barony of Dudley 1070-1757.* Hemingway's research concentrates on the history of Dudley and therefore covers specific matters which are beyond the remit of this saga, but make fascinating reading for those wishing to delve deeper.[194]

---

193 *The Tudors*, p.187.

194 John Hemingway, *An Illustrated Chronicle of the Castle and Barony of Dudley 1070-1757.*

Robert Dudley (Earl of Leicester as granted by Elizabeth I)

Northumberland's offspring worked closely together as Protestant Reformers. These Dudleys helped speed up the pace of the spread of Protestantism, which included being influential in Stratford, where Shakespeare's father, a Catholic Jesuit schoolmaster, took himself to the safety of the continent. Robert Dudley was Northumberland's younger son but this line of the family could not avoid being discredited by their father.

The executions of the Guildfords was in the past when in 1560 Robert Dudley's wife Amy was found dead with a broken neck at the bottom of a staircase. Many assumed that wishing to be free to court Elizabeth, Robert had ordered Amy's murder. This accusation made no sense because a royal marriage would have been unthinkably political in such circumstances. The death was judged to be accidental by the coroner's jury.

People began to accept Calvinism (it was not yet described as Anglicanism). Protestant clergy married and grew hair and beards. Robert Dudley felt that the Church of England needed to be purified of remaining Catholic superstitions and it was from such belief that Puritanism emerged whereby extreme Protestants took their own stance. The resulting *Thirty-Nine Articles of Religion* in 1563 sought to define the difference between the Church of England and the Catholic Church.[195] Robert Dudley had joined the Council and the Bishop of Salisbury the year before in accord with John Jewels' published *Apology or Answer in Defence of the Church of England.* Dudley, along with Huntingdon and Lord Burghley, had believed that Presbyterianism was right, that superstition and Popish values were spiritually flawed, but not all Puritans were Presbyterians.

James Harington's brother-in-law was Henry Sidney (1529-1586), who married Lady Mary Dudley of Warwick (1535-1586). Their Sidney descendants became a new line of Earls of Leicester for generations to come. William Lord Hastings, cousin and sometime friend of Edward 24th Dudley Baron, married Katherine Neville yet fought her brother; his fate was execution. The Earls of Leicester and the Hastings family were connected to Ashby-de-la-Zouch in Leicestershire. Hastings had meant to outdo the Greys of Groby with major

195 *The Tudors*, pp.171, 179, 186, 195-196, 228. John Jewels, *Apology or Answer in Defence of the Church of England* (1562). Thirty-nine Articles of Religion (1563).

architectural improvements there. Henry Hastings was a Puritan revolutionary at a time when Ashby was renowned as a religious centre.[196] Lord Leicester helped Thomas Cartwright, a leading Puritan. Under the Anglican Church in the 1570s, the Privy Council was revised and new blood brought in; traditional conservative aristocrats were reduced in number. Militant Protestants formed an inner circle, which included Sir Walter Mildmay and Sir Francis Walshingham. The Puritan Vicar of Sedgley, William Fenner, lost his living despite having persuaded his Puritan allies to stay within the Church of England.[197] Puritanism declined somewhat in the 1580s.

Edward Sutton 4th, Dudley Baron 24th (1516-1586)

Grandson of the 20th Baron and his wife Cecily Grey, Edward was a soldier, who lived through the reigns of four of the five Tudor monarchs (Henry VIII, Edward VI, Mary I and Elizabeth I). In Ireland in 1536, he served under Leonard Grey (born 1479), known to him as uncle.[198] Unfortunately, Leonard Grey was beheaded for treason at the Tower of London on 28 July 1541. Being a marshall, he had been created 1st Viscount Grane in the Peerage of Ireland in 1535 and served as the Lord Deputy of Ireland from 1536 to 1540. Henry VIII instructed Grey to command an army against Irish rebels (who would not acknowledge Henry's supremacy as Head of the Church of England) and they were meant to renounce the Pope. This was a dangerous mission: his job was to enforce obedience to Henry, which rebels pretended to do in Galway but the King rapidly noticed:

> "Their oaths, submissions and indentures were not worth a farthing, since they did not give hostages."

Lambert Palace Library holds records of Grey's later progression through Ireland, which included Togher Crogham. He travelled out of a strong and dangerous pass called Balleighgeran and camped at the abbey of Killcormoke,

---

196 Adam Fox, 'Religious Satire in English Towns 1570-1640' in *The Reformation in the English Towns 1500*-1640, ed. Patrick Collinson and John Craig (Edinburgh, 1998), ch. 12, pp.221-240, also 241-335.

197 *Kings and Queens of the British Isles*, ed. Thomas Cussans, *The Times* (London, 2015), illus., maps.

198 'Leonard Grey, 1st Viscount Grane' (2004). *https://en.wikipedia.org/wiki/Leonard_Grey,_1st_Viscount_Grane* [accessed 6 July 2020]. Fn. 3 Lyons (2004).

where he was victualled by friends. This suggests he was both fearless and sociable. He dutifully observed robbing and spoiling and accepted sterling. In the county of Limericke he faced extreme peril. Dated October 1540, the results of an examination of about 70 accounts against Lord Grey, overseen by his predecessor Sir Anthony St. Leger, were sent to Henry VIII. They comprised a great book, every leaf subscribed by Sir Anthony, upon receipt of which Grey's fate was sealed.[199] A sweating sickness broke out in 1543, multitudes died, which Henry turned to his advantage, but Gerald of the House of Kildare escaped the King's wrath, Grey was blamed and attainted and that was how he was brought to the scaffold. His young nephew was Earl of Kildare.

From 1546, Edward served in Scotland. It is thought that he was Governor of Hume Castle in 1547 after it was taken by English forces, but he was captured by the Scots when they retook the castle in 1548.[200] [201] The Earl of Shrewsbury was asked by the Privy Council in 1550 to exchange Sutton for French hostages to the value of £200.[202]

Lord Quondam had died in 1553. The barony had been with (Northumberland) John 23rd Dudley Baron since 1537 but Edward did not become 24th Baron until 1554; barony years are easily confused with birth years. He was knighted and contemporary sources refer to him as Sir Edward. With the title restored to his senior line, he returned to Dudley. Whatever emotion he felt in finding King Henry VIII's Protestant damage there, he could not reclaim rights on behalf of the Priory monks or restore the castle chapel, but he succeeded in getting back castle land and 'Old Park', the area between Dudley Castle and Burnt Tree in the Parish of Sedgley that had once been baronial possessions. In 1563 a deed described land leased to William Grove as part of the Dudley lord's 'domaynes'. Northumberland seemed to have eliminated previous Catholic elements and had been responsible for having

199 Lambeth Palace Library, MS. 601, p.35. Calendar of the Carew Manuscripts preserved in the Archiepiscopal Library at Lambeth, ed. J.S. Brewer and W. Bullen (1867-73), vol. 1 of 6, document 149, 10p., (not held at the National Archives). [Accessed 2 September 2017].

200 BHO, 'Parishes: Dudley' in *A History of the County of Worcester: Vol. 3,* orig. pub. by Victoria County History (London, 1913), pp.90-105. *http://www.british-history.ac.uk/vch/worcs/vol3* [accessed 21 November 2016]. Fns. 89-94 Lives of Barons Edward Sutton Dudley 8th and 9th. (There are differing ways of counting).

201 'Dud Dudley and Abraham Darby, Forging new Links'. (Retrieved by Black Country Society, 28 May 2015).

202 Parliament, *Acts of the Privy Council*, John Roche Dasent, HMSO (1890), vol. 2, p.21 (named Edward Dudley).

the Sharrington Range designed in the 1550s. Sir William Sharrington created it for the 23rd Baron to satisfy simple Protestant taste in new architectural style. Sharrington is perhaps better known as the architect of Laycock Abbey and for his imprisonment due to fraud (counterfeiting coins).

From 1556-58, Edward 24th Baron was lieutenant of Hampnes in Picardy.[203] Lady Katherine (born Brydges) was his first wife; they married in 1556 and she died ten years later. Katherine was the daughter of John Brydges, 1st Baron Chandon and Elizabeth (born Grey of Wilton). It is thought that she helped with local matters relating to the manor and honor of Dudley, especially when Edward was away. In 1564, she seems to have transferred the 'Olde Parke' to Hugh Liddiatt of Halesowen and William Harrison of Dudley. She predeceased her husband by 20 years and was buried in St. Edmund's Church, the castle church in Dudley.

Edward's second wife was Jane (born Stanley), daughter of Edward Stanley, 3rd Earl of Derby and Lady Dorothy (born Howard). The arms of Stanley had a quartering of Woodville, possibly from the time of 1st Lord Derby. Jane was mother of Edward's eldest son and heir, also called Edward (25th Dudley Baron); their other son was John (1569-1644/5). Both Edwards were direct ancestors in this saga, cousins to Northumberland 23rd Dudley Baron.

The children had a stepmother when Edward 24th Baron married his third wife in 1570, Mary (Marie, daughter of William, 1st Baron Howard, a high admiral, sister of another whose wife was the Queen's cousin and intimate friend). Five years later, the 24th Baron entertained Queen Elizabeth I at Dudley Castle.[204] It's easy to imagine their Protestant conversations. Edward died on 12 July 1586. The following year, his widow Mary married Richard Mompesson of Salisbury, Wiltshire. Lady Marie died on 21 August 1600 (aged 52, if @RichardMompessonMP is correct). Her monument, with Richard adjacent, is in St. Margaret's Church, Westminster, at the eastern corner of the south aisle where an enclosure forms a vestibule to both the vestry and church:[205]

---

203 Parliament, *Acts of the Privy Council for the Age of Elizabeth* (1558-1603). *www.british-history.ac.uk* (unseen).

204 'John de Dudley subarticle Edmund Dudley' in *Dictionary of National Biography*, Smith, Elder & Co. (London, 1885-1900).

205 Walter Thornbury, 'St Margaret's Westminster', in *Old and New London: Volume 3* (London, 1878), pp.567-576. British History Online, *http://www.british-history.ac.uk/old-new-london/vol3/pp567-576* [accessed 5 October 2017].

> "The largest and finest of these [monuments] is one in the Jacobean style, to Marie, Lady Dudley, a daughter of the Lord High Admiral, Lord Howard of Effingham, and grand-daughter of Thomas, second Duke of Norfolk. She died in the year 1600, having married first Edward Sutton, Lord Dudley, and secondly Richard Montpesson who erected the tomb. The husband is represented in a kneeling attitude, the lady recumbent. Her monument, which bears a striking resemblance to the 'Founder's Tomb' in the Charterhouse Chapel, is beautifully adorned with colour and armorial bearings."

And:

> "She was firste married to Edw. Sutton Lo: Dudley & after to Rich: Montpesson Esq: who in the memorie of her vertues & laste testimony of his love, erected this monument. She slept in Christ Jesus in the yere of our Lord 1600 & the 21 of Aug attending the joyful day of her resvrrection."

To the right, there is another tribute to her as Lady Marie, the 4th Baron Edward's third wife Mary Howarde:

> "Here lieth entombed, Marie La Dudley, daughter of Will Lo: Howarde of Effingha, in his tyme Lo: High Admyrail of Englande, Lo: Chaberlayne & Lo: Privy. She was grandchild of Thomas D. of Norff the 2 of that svrnae: & sister to Chares Howarde, Erle of Nott. Lo High Admyrail of England by whose prosperous direccio thorough the goodn of God, in defending the whole fleete of Spayne was defeated & discomfited."

Edward Sutton 5th, Dudley 25th Baron (1567-1643)

Edward Sutton, 25th Dudley, lived through the reigns of three monarchs (Elizabeth I, James I and Charles I). His arranged marriage to Theodosia Harington (1565-1650), daughter of Sir James of Exton, MP and lawyer, took place when he was only 14 years old on 12 June 1581.[206] By the 16th century,

206 *History of Parliament: The House of Commons 1558-1603*, ed. P.W. Hasler (1981). *http://www.historyofparliamentonline.org/volume/1558-1603/* [accessed 15 October 2017].

the main branches of the Haringtons were landowners in Leicestershire, Rutland and Lincolnshire. Ridlington in Rutland was Sir James Harington's estate. Only one year before his marriage, Edward had been educated at Lincoln College, Oxford, aged 13 and then he succeeded his father as Dudley Baron in 1586. This made him a major landowner with estates including many coal workings and a furnace at Himley. With Theodosia he had five legitimate children. Their daughter Anne Sutton Dudley was to marry Hans Meinhardt von Schonberg (1582-1616), Palatine Ambassador to England. Her distant cousin had been the Rt. Rev. William Dudley, Bishop of Durham (d.1532 if this date is correct). The main one of three 16th century English palinates was Durham. The Bishop of Durham, brother of Edmund (b.1425), in that case was an earlier Rt. Rev. William de Sutton (1431-1483).

Mistress Elizabeth Tomlinson (1567-1629)

Direct ancestor Elizabeth Tomlinson was permanently in Edward 25th Baron's life, mother to their estimated eleven illegitimate children. She was the daughter of Agnes, whose maiden name was Dues (alt. Orres, D'Orres), and William Millington Tomlinson (alt. Tomlenson, Tumlenson, 1540-1609) a Dudley collier, both 15th generation direct ancestors within this saga. Coal was used for heating forges and hearths then, not for smelting iron.[207] There is pride in being a coalminer and this is very much acknowledged. He might have had a supervisory role under Edward's direction because there was much more to the Tomlinson family than the Lyttletons probably knew.

The line goes back to William Myllington Tomlinson who was married to Agnes (born de Saint Liz, 1430-1460). Several wives of this family were named Agnes. Next down was Agnes Sotherton (1464-1502) who was married to Thomas Millington Tomlinson (1460-1508). Quite a few facts are known of this Sotherton line on family history websites such as Geni:

> "William I Sotherton, born about 1440, is the earliest member of this family at Holme-on-Spalding-Moor, County York, from whom a direct line can be traced; and for a continuous period of nearly three centuries they seem to have been the wealthiest family of the parish, except the

207 Carl Higgs, *Sedgley Men of Iron: Dud Dudley and Abraham Darby Keeping it in the Family!* Illus. *http://www.sedgleymanor.com/people/dud_dudley.html* [accessed 19 March 2016].

> Constables and later the Landales, who were the lords and proprietors of the manor. During the fifteenth, sixteenth and seventeenth centuries the Sotherons were substantial yeomen, farming extensive estates which they held by leases from the manor of Holme; and as early as 1585 they began to be also freehold owners of lands there which they acquired by purchase."

A William Sothern's will exists in Latin from 1509 in the Prerogative and Exchequer of York Wills.[208] There is also a record of Sir Thomas II, a priest at Beverly, County York, whose will mentioned a large number of relations named Sotheron and Tomlinson. This family are variously called Millington or Tomlinson, with each sometimes an alias for the other both ways. As for Millington the parish in the union of Pocklington, 16 miles east of York, four ancient roads meet here. About half a mile north-east of the village lie foundations of a circular temple and two oblong buildings. Roman pavements, tiles, coins and various other relics of antiquity have been discovered there.

As for Elizabeth Tomlinson's mother (born Dues or Orres), Ancestry.com maps the name Orre(s) to originate from just below Anglesey in Wales, a beautiful coastline as anyone who has visited Beaumaris on the Menai Strait will know. In Welsh, Sant Dewi means Saint David. USA statistics of 1940 showed the main occupations of people with the surname Orre as:

"Women	Clerk	100%
Men	Laborer	47%
	Farmer	39%
	Operator	16%."

Elizabeth Tomlinson, Edward Sutton Dudley and their children shared their lives together in Dudley. Edward must have loved Elizabeth dearly and he provided generously for his illegitimate offspring. This saga continues down with their daughter Jane (1591-1656) Sutton Dudley's line. She was sister to Dud and grandmother Persehouse to John Darby Junior of Coalbrookdale.

---

208 *https://www.ancestry.com/last-name-meaning/orre?geo-lang=en-US&msockid=0a2af695e46560bb2831e09be534616c*

Trouble in Westminster

Sir John Lyttleton's eldest son was Sir Gilbert Lyttleton MP (c.1540-1599), the man who insulted Elizabeth Tomlinson in 1592. Theodosia (born Harington) was Edward's only wife, decided by parental arrangement when he was only 14 years old. In the background to this case hung lasting rivalry over Prestwood land, Edward's most bitter feud of all. Lyttleton knew Dudley had a growing family with Elizabeth. At the Star Chamber, he attempted to discredit Edward by claiming that he was living with, "a lewd and infamous woman, a base collier's daughter." His other allegation was that Dudley had abandoned Theodosia in London, "without provision of sustenance."

Edward 25th Baron spent much of his life in indebtedness, constantly pressed to pay his dues. The Dudley Estate was in difficulty under both Edwards. The 24th Baron's will had left provision to pay all proceeds of his iron works to his creditors for 21 years. This left the 25th Baron without means to pay an annuity that should have gone to his brother John. By 1593, the estate was in the hands of sequestrators, the same year Edward 25th took his seat in the House of Lords, having made no known contribution to the Commons even though he could have done so from 1584.[209] Money was constantly lacking to support Theodosia. She was cohabiting in London with their children, Ferdinando, Mary, Anne and an infant, which meant she needed money for her bills and boarding costs. Each child should have received yearly annual amounts from Edward.

Thus Edward inherited his father's immense debts. The terms of his marriage had been meant to bring wealth but he had little money. The Privy Council ordered Dudley to pay Theodosia an allowance, which he failed to do because of his difficulties. In August 1597 he was sent to Fleet Prison, a notorious London gaol by the side of the River Fleet, although after a few days he was released on condition that he was to pay maintenance of £100 yearly for his wife, plus £20 for each legitimate child. In less than 18 months he was back before the Privy Council, having got into arrears. Edward seemed to be a kind, ill-fated man, drawn to Elizabeth for life. The Tomlinsons had calibre, colliers like her father would be the might of the Black Country. The Baron was required to pay for his legitimate children's needs and was also asked to repay a loan to Sir John Harington.

209 *History of Parliament: The House of Commons 1558-1603*, ed. P.W. Hasler.

The friction between the Dudleys and the Lyttletons had been going on for years with lawlessness occurring on both sides. Both men were MPs, perhaps politics provoked them more. The Lyttletons brought a later Star Chamber suit against Dudley, consequently he was heavily fined for rioting and cattle-stealing. The feud between the families explained a conspiracy between Dudley and the Staffordshire High Sheriff Thomas Whorwood, John Sutton Dudley's father-in-law, in 1597. To secure the election of a county seat for John, Edward's younger brother, who was standing in opposition to Sir Edward Lyttleton of Pillaton Hall, was a close ally of Robert Devereux, 2nd Earl of Essex. At this election, Dudley himself shouted his 'voice vote' for his brother, "with great and loud voice." The sheriff allowed the vote but in his subsequent Star Chamber action pointed out that a peer of the realm had no voice in the election of a knight of the shire.[210] As a peer, Dudley should have had no part in elections to the Commons, Whorwood was right in this regard. However, such a constitutional principle may never have been argued before. This was a major political event for Edward. His chicanery and bad manners seemed scandalous to those in the land who thought themselves his better. Sir Christopher Blount, Essex's step-father, was offended by being placed below Sutton on the election indenture; Essex's mother thought it outrageous too. They caused Edward to be brought to the Privy Council where Lyttleton mostly blamed Whorwood for allowing a blank election return.[211]

The 24th and 25th Barons were ironmasters, plagued with serious debts yet their coalfields, mineral and ore sources in Dudley were the early foundation of the Industrial Revolution and the Sutton Dudleys were enterprising men. This was massively beneficial to the descendants of Frances, Edward 25th's granddaughter, in later centuries and also influential to great achievements down Tomlinson family lines.

Robert Dudley and other suitors seeking the hand of Elizabeth I in marriage

Robert Dudley and Elizabeth Tudor had been childhood friends. Later, as her suitor, he leased the demesnes of Grafton Regis, the old home of the

210 *History of Parliament: The House of Commons 1558-1603*, ed. P.W. Hasler. J. Hawarde, *Les Reportes del Cases in Camera Stellata*, passim; *Erdswicke's Surv. Staffs*, 374 seq.

211 *History of Parliament: Constituencies 1558-1603 – Staffordshire. http://www.historyofparliament.org/volume/1588-1603/constituencies/staffordshire* [accessed 15 October 2020].

Woodvilles. In 1551-3, £170 was spent on repairs to the house followed by £450 in 1553-4. He called it his Queen's "stately honor house", but Elizabeth I only went there three times, in 1564, 68 and 75. Her latter visit was to hold council meetings. Minor further expenditure was needed each time, costing £396.[212]

An original letter by Langham can be found at the British Library, St. Pancras. It has a romantic slant as the letter records the journey of Queen Elizabeth I to Kenilworth Castle in 1575 and contains what is considered to be the best description known of an Elizabethan garden. Langham's surname spelling has changed to Laneham in modern times. Robert Dudley was inspired to provide a beautiful garden at Kenilworth in preparation for the Queen's visit. He planned to court her, and to ask for her hand in marriage one final time. English Heritage referred to the letter in order to recreate a complete Elizabethan garden experience at the castle. To achieve this, Elizabethan literature was thoroughly researched and the garden was faithfully and devotedly reproduced and opened to the public in 2009. The project was supported by the Wolfson Foundation.[213]

Robert had been a suitor for Elizabeth's hand in marriage from early in her reign, even being her preferred choice. Sir William Cecil realised that such a marriage could undermine his own influence. However, Elizabeth allowed no-one to choose on her behalf, she felt decisions concerning her succession were her royal prerogative and enforced this opinion in 1579 when she banished Leicester and Pembroke temporarily from the Presence Chamber – a chamber for private contact between only monarch and courtier, a harsh punishment.

Mary Fitton (alt. Fytton, c.1578-1647) was linked in some way to Tettenhall (near Dudley). She was maid of honour to Queen Elizabeth I. A beautiful yet volatile court lady, Mary was thought to be the original dark lady that inspired Shakespeare's characters, although this assumption is

---

212 BHO, 'Grafton Regis' in *A History of the County of Northampton: Vol. 5*, The Hundred of Cleley. (London, orig. pub. by Victoria County History, 2002), pp.142-176. *https://www.britishhistory.ac.uk/vch/northants/vols/pp142-176* [accessed 3 June 2020]. Fn. 148 *King's Works*, iv, 93. Fn. 149 *Cal. S.P. Dom*, 1566-1579, 339-340; below, econ. Hist. Fn. 151 *Acts of P.C.*, 1571-1575, 400-402, ibid. 1575-1577, 3-4.

213 BHO, 'Parishes: Kenilworth' in *A History of the County of Warwick*: *Vol. 6*, Knightlow Hundred, ed. L.F. Salzman (London, 1951), pp.132-143 *http://www.british history.ac.uk/vch/warks/vol6/pp132-143* [accessed 11 October 2017].

now much in doubt. Gawsworth Hall in Macclesfield, Cheshire was built in 1480, then in the diocese of Lichfield, on the site of an early Norman house. It was the home of Sir Edward and Lady Fitton, parents of the said Mary, their youngest daughter. The Fittons spent a fortune (£10 million in 2019 money) including expenditure on a massive Tudor garden, ever hoping that Elizabeth would visit. Would one of their two sons court the Queen? Mary had a scandalous affair with William Herbert, 3rd Earl of Pembroke, which resulted in both William and Mary being dismissed from court. She had become pregnant but lost her baby boy and Pembroke was briefly jailed at Fleet prison in 1601.[214] [215] Also, Mary was linked to Vice-Admiral Sir Richard Leveson and Sir William Knollys.

The Danish royal family

The Danish royal family became relevant to this saga. Following Frederick II's royal marriage to Queen Sophie on 20 July 1572, his true love, Anne Cordfitzdatter, wedded Oluf Krognos at the Church of Our Lady, Copenhagen on 11 January 1573. Her bridegroom died 25 June 1573 the same year.[216] [217]

There is evidence that Anne was a Danish county sheriff:

> "Of high nobility, Anne Hardenberg was chambermaid to Queen Dorothea 1557-71, and here she got to know King Frederik II (King from 1559) who fell in love with her, and wanted to marry her, but this met widespread opposition. In 1572 she married Councillor of the Realm, Oluf Mouritsen Krognos, who died after only six months marriage. She lived at her dowry Bregentved and managed to keep her husband's family at distance with the help of the royal family."

Queen Sophie studied chemistry and astronomy and visited Danish astronomer Tycho Brahe (1546-1601) at his observatory on the island of

214 The National Archives, Court of Star Chamber STAC 5/H25/2.

215 Letters of Robert Cecil to George Carew (London, 1864), p.65.

216 *Ann Hardenberg*, www.zoominfo.com *http://www.zoominfo.com/p/Ann-Hardenberg/1228709821* [accessed 8 February 2017].

217 Female County Sheriffs in the Kingdom of Denmark and Norway (including parts of that is now Southern Sweden), Danish County Sheriffs. *www.Guide2women.com/womeninpower/Danish_County_Sheriffs.htm* [accessed 8 February 2017].

Hven. There were connections between Dudley gentry and the royal family that could have spread new astronomical ideas but scarcely did.[218] Elizabeth I was familiar with Frederick II of Denmark but there was no romance between them. The English maintained close contact with the kingdoms of Denmark and Sweden through trade in Baltic timber and fish. English towns generally provided economic trading and functioned as manufacturing places. In Worcester ideas flourished amongst receptive cloth workers because they used the same networks as traders. The counties of Worcestershire, Northamptonshire and Buckinghamshire tried to establish appropriate wage rates for various trades.[219]

At the English theatre, alien stereotypes were presented, for example, of Danes being lazy, but consider the hard work of Tycho, who catalogued the sky and accurately pinpointed over 770 fixed stars with simple instruments before there were telescopes. Frederick II supported Tycho as a friend and allegedly loved hunting, feasts, women and too much wine.

A majority of family historians record Princess Catherine of Denmark and Norway (1580-1675) as Frederick and Sophie's legitimate child, although Catherine was ostracised from the family due to their objections that she was marrying beneath her status. Any differences between Catherine and Queen Anne may have persisted but with both sisters living in England they could have overcome earlier problems. Another sibling, Augusta, was born in April 1580, the same year as Catherine's birth, which is biologically possible as they could have been twins. There are more questions than answers. Could Catherine's first marriage to Simeone Leete of Eversden have been Sophie's idea? Was Sophie known to be astute at arranging lucrative marriages? Were the Leetes perhaps socially higher than the Turleys? Maybe Sophie had chosen an unknown other potential husband whom Catherine had declined? It is unclear which of Catherine's two husbands caused the Danish royal family to isolate her. When Sophie died (1631 in Nykoping), she was said to be the wealthiest woman in Northern Europe.[220] A Simeone Leete, son

218 Ian Mortimer, *The Time Traveller*, pp.113, 115, 120, 143.

219 *The Tudors*, p.176.

220 Sharon L. Jansen, *The Monstrous Regiment of Women: Sophie of Mecklenburg*, (September 2015), *http://www.monstrousregimentofwomen.com/2015/sopie-of-mecklenburg* [accessed 17 April 2016].

of Robert, was baptised on 23 June 1573 in Great Eversden.[221] The estate of Great Eversden Manor included land in Little Eversden and elsewhere. A later Robert Leete, in his will of 1836, gave £200 for the maintenance of the Eversden Chapel and its minister and £100 for poor members of the congregation. Stephen Leete similarly left £100 in 1837 and Lydia Leete gave £300 in her will, proved 1854, towards the purchase and enfranchisement of the manse plus £100 to Addenbrooke's Hospital for the admission of a patient from Little Eversden.[222] These Leetes were generous people, evidently with means. The then Walsingham, a Justice of the Peace in the uprising of 1381, was killed in Ely and his estate at Great Eversden was plundered. Eventually, Sir Pain Tiptoft bought the manor.

The Tiptofts' connection to Dudley could be highly relevant, Joyce Tiptoft (1430-1485) married Edmund Sutton (b.1525), they were 18th generation ancestors within this saga. She was descended from Sir Pain (alt. Payne) MP (1351-1413). Her brother was 1st Earl of Worcester and her mother's name was Joyce (b. Cherleton, 1403-1446). When a Joyce Tiptoft and her husband died in the 1440s, Eversden Manor and a tenement there were called Courthoses. Whether 'court' here bears any meaning to the legal word 'leete' is probable. Could Simeone Leete have come from a family of lawyers? Name researchers cite feudal legal connections. There was a Letia of Cambridge recorded in the *Hundred Rolls* of 1273.[223]

---

221 Joseph Leete, *The Family of Leet[e] with special reference to the Genealogy of Joseph Leete, Esq., F.S.S. Chevelier De La Legion d'honneur, South Norwood, Surrey*, collected by Charles Bridger (friend and assistant of Stephen Tucker, Somerset Herald, College of Arms, London), (c. 1881), pp.ix, 32, illus. Joseph Leete, *The Family of Leete* (Classic reprint series). *https://www.forgottenbooks.com* [accessed 26 May 2020]. (The ink was yellow with age. Registers between 1600 and 1700 had been destroyed by fire or had disappeared through causes unknown to the vicar or oldest inhabitant). Baptism record, Eversden Magna, first page of old chronicle. (Joseph Leete could have been Simeon's grandfather. Magna was one of two ancient parishes, the other was Parva. The Leetes of Eversden were in the Herald's visitation of Cambridge in 1619).

222 BHO, 'Parishes: Great and Little Eversden', by Diane K. Bolton, in *A History of the County of Cambridge and the Isle of Ely: Vol. 5*, ed. C R Elrington (London, 1973), pp.59-68. *http://www.british-history.ac.uk/vch/cambs/vol5/pp59-68* [accessed 3 July 2020]. Fn. 52 Cal. Close, 1369-1374, 604; 1374-1377, 110. Fn. 53 Cambs Village Docs. 27. Fn. 74 Queen's Coll. Mun. MS cal. Deed 5 November 1491; Cal. Inq. p.m. Henry VII, iii, p.593. Fn. 311 *Char. Digest Cambs.* H.C. 433-516, pp.20-21 (1867-1868), iii (2); Char. Com. Unrep. Vol. 14, pp.351, 353-354, Char. Com. Files.

223 *Hundredorum Rolls* (1273). *https://www.houseofnames.com/blogs/Hundred-Rolls* [accessed 20 July 2020].

Princess Anne of Denmark and Norway's royal wedding of 1589 to King James VI of Scotland was a ceremony conducted in French so that both parties could understand. Anne also spoke German and was brought up in the Lutheran religion but converted to Roman Catholicism during the 1590s.[224] [225] Denmark and Sweden embraced their Lutheran Reformation whereas Scotland did not follow these northern choices, but the English Reformation model played a big part in the Scottish Reformation.[226] Anne's father Frederick II died the year before their wedding. He had been unable to gain dominance of the Baltic in the Seven Years' War of the North (1560s-1570). Nevertheless, his grip on Baltic trade secured Danish prosperity in later years. He fought his cousin Eric XIV of Sweden but eventually Danish power was overcome. Frederick was a Renaissance ruler with military ideals, he was said to be hot-headed. He was also defined by ambition, courage and vanity. He had an amicable side though, having been friends of German Princes in his youth. This was evident again when the Treaty of Mozhalstk pleased Ivan of Russia. Frederick's younger brother Magnus of Holstein supported Protestantism and received the Knight of the Garter from Elizabeth I. Frederick might have relied on customs revenues as much as Elizabeth yet this income was not raised in England until the reign of James I.[227]

If it was known where Catherine of Denmark could have met her first husband Simeone, it might help unravel the circumstances that brought Catherine and her second husband John Turley of this saga together, because in 1600 Catherine wedded John in Sedgley (near Dudley) where she was thereafter known as Catherine, Princess of Turley. The Tudor dynasty ended in 1603 when Queen Elizabeth I was succeeded by the first Stuart monarch, James I of England (VI of Scotland), whose Queen consort was Catherine's sister Anne.

---

224 Tudor Times, 'Anne of Denmark Life Story'. *http://tudortimes.co.uk/people/anne-of-denmark-life-story* [accessed 27 September 2016].

225 English Monarchs, *Anne of Denmark 12 December 1574-2 March 1619* (2004-2008), illus. *http://www.englishmonarchs.co.uk/* [accessed 6 July 2020].

226 Adams, Simon and P. Collinson, eds., 'Britain Europe and the World' in *Short History of the British Isles: the Sixteenth Century* (Oxford, 2002), ch.6, p.28.

227 *Encyclopaedia Britannica*, editors. 'Frederick II King of Denmark and Norway'. *http://www.britannica.com* [accessed 27 September 2016].

Chapter 5

Surprising Stuarts?

ELIZABETH TOMLINSON'S older sister is generally referred to as Ann, although that name could have been misread as Joan or interchanged with the name Agnes. Her line is believed to include a prominent descendant, former United States President Richard Nixon, which means that the Tomlinsons receive attention from genealogists and family historians in the US, leading to scrutiny of Ann, her husband, her sister Elizabeth Tomlinson, their parents and the Sutton Dudleys. When Nixon was impeached, some described him as a realist.

The Privy Council wrote to Worcestershire Assizes in July 1598, demanding action against two of Gilbert Lyttleton's sons, Stephen and John, who had attacked John Sutton and his retainers. The Dudleys had already argued over a property dispute. It was easy to find wrongdoings in Sir Gilbert Lyttleton's family because his relations were connected with the Gunpowder Plot of 1605. Stephen Lyttleton was one of the most prominent members of the Midlands' Catholic community, Humphrey Lyttleton was involved as well. Stephen owned a new home, Holbeche House, near Kingswinford, where the plotters took shelter, having stolen supplies from Warwick Castle on 6 November as well as gun powder and weapons from Hewell Grange the next day. When a posse found them there, mostly killed or wounded, the survivors were tried and executed.[228]

---

228 Lucy Aikin, *Memoirs of the Court of James the First* (1822).

James VI of Scotland (1st of England from 1603-1625)

Not everyone believed in black magic but unfortunately King James and Anne both did; he was called "the wisest fool in Christendom." An otherwise talented scholar with an enquiring mind and interest in science, he chose to apply his intellect to writing *Daemonologie* in three parts between 1597-1599 (a work that covered magic, sorcery and witchcraft). James was absorbed with how these evils could be eliminated.[229]

Danish State Visit, 1606

Splendid and grand Danish vessels brought King Christian IV of Denmark and Norway (1577-1648) on a royal state visit to London in July 1606.[230] Shakespeare would have played three times to royalty; a major ceremonial episode which seems to have escaped the attention of historians. Heavy drinking at the Jacobean court, influenced by alleged Danish fondness for alcohol, displeased James I as he disliked liquor. Christian's behaviour was said to have disgusted Sir John Harington. Theodosia resided in London, she could well have been there or aware of gossip. Her estranged husband, Dudley 25th Baron, was in his prime at this time. If Christian was as promiscuous as his reputation, would he really have criticised Catherine? As for her sister, the Queen, now living in London, would Anne not have welcomed her sister Catherine's company? The court scene certainly conjures up a social spectacle of colour and drama. Anne could be capable and cultured; she commissioned Queen's House, Greenwich, although the ceiling depicting 'Astronomy', as a figure in white, holding up an open book to the stars, had to wait for the sophisticated taste of Charles I's wife Henrietta Maria of France.

Anne of Denmark

James I and Christian IV were brothers-in-law. Anne was a distant cousin to James as well as his wife, which means her sister Catherine was his cousin too. Scotland and Denmark had been on good terms since the marriage of Margaret of Denmark to James II (of Scotland) in 1469, a connection that evidently went back generations. His Protestant bride maximised James'

229 King James Stuart, *Daemonologie* (1597-99), 3 parts. [Unseen].

230 James Shapiro, *1606, Shakespeare and the Year of Lear*, (PLACE, 2016).

chances of acceding to the wealthier English throne. James and Anne married young, she was at most 15 years old but Elizabeth I had favoured the match: bolstering a strong northern Protestant alliance was perfect for both sides of the arrangement.[231] Catherine is omitted from records because the Danish royal family ostracised her for marrying beneath her status.

When Princess Anne entered London, she had received a warm welcome:

> "The night-bell man of Pickadilly to the Princess of Denmark. Welcome great princess to this lovely place."

From the same source:[232]

> "The genealogies of the high-born Prince & Princess George and Anne of Denmark, &c. shewing the lineal descent of these two noble and illustrious families: with their matches, issue, times of death, places of sepulchre, impresses, devices, &c..."

Queen Anne's Almshouses, in the Parish of Newport Paganell, Buckinghamshire, located at 34-42 St. John's Street, are a clue to a medieval link with Dudleys through the name Paganell. There are various spellings in the literature. The almshouses were originally founded in 1287 at St. John's Hospital. In 1615 they were re-founded for elderly and poor persons of the town by deed of a charter granted by James I. It directed that the name be changed to Queen Anne's Hospital, the property seems to have been in the King's ownership.[233] [234] [235] Choosing to grace it with Anne's name might indicate centuries old kinship. The couple were distant cousins after all. Newport Pagnell Historical Society tell of an Iron Bridge (1810) and an ancient stone house (the Vicarage until 1875). At the rear of that abode is a medieval stone wall, once part of a Tudor

---

231 *Tudor Times*, 'Anne of Denmark: Life Story: Family & Childhood' (November, 2016), ch. 1, p.8. *https://historycollection.com* [accessed 24 July 2020].

232 *Early English Books Online* (EEBO), source SFX. Source record 1000 + nine zeros, 661319, 666883.

233 F.W. Bull, *A History of Newport Pagnell* (1900).

234 N. Pevsner and E. Williamson, *Buckinghamshire*, 2nd ed., (1994), p.579. (Building of England Series).

235 Historic England, *Queen Anne's Almshouses*, Grade II Listed Building, 1st listed 17 February 2000. List entry number 1380128. *https://historicengland.org.uk* [accessed 9 September 2020].

structure. Almshouses nearby comprised the fourth of such premises on the site. There is an interesting plaque above a front window dated 1615, dedicating the hospital to the people of the town from Queen Anne, wife of James I.[236] UK Genealogy Archives refers to three suites of almshouses and explains that the town stands on the confluence of the rivers Ouse and Looat. At first the manor was held by FitzAusculph (Fitzansculf) but soon took its name from the Paganel family, owners of the manor during the reign of William Rufus. The castle and a Cluniac Priory, which they also founded, had similarities to Dudley. Tickford Abbey later occupied the priory's spot in Newport Pagnell.

Camden described the castle before it had fallen into decay as "a place of great strength."[237] It passed from the Paganels to the Someries. Newport Paganel was part of the dower lands of Lucy de Somery. The oldest part of the church was the porch built in the reign of Edward III. Queen Anne's Hospital was founded circa 1280 by John de Somerie and its old stone building was replaced with brick in 1892. If the town had legal or religious relevance to James and Anne, it is interesting to learn that it was a seat of assizes in the reigns of Henry III until Henry VI and belonged to the diocese of Oxford.[238]

Sir Fernando Sutton Dudley (1588-1621) heir of 25th Dudley Baron attended the investiture in 1610 of Prince Henry Frederick Stuart, eldest son and heir of James I and Anne. Thereby Henry was made Prince of Wales and Earl of Chester. It was an important occasion because Scottish and English titles of the heir apparent became united for the first time. A masque and a pageant took place, the kind of entertainment Queen Anne adored. She must have been so happy with the sword she received encrusted with diamonds.[239] [240] Evidently, Ferdinando and most probably his wife Lady Honora Seymour (d.1620) were favoured at court (due to their Dudley connection), therefore

---

236 Newport Pagnell Historical Society, *The Old Vicarage and Queen Anne's Hospital* (2018).

237 AncestryLibraryEdition.co.uk, *England Topographical Dictionary, Newport-Pagnell*, pp.32 of 39. *https://www.ancestrylibraryedition.co.uk/interactive/7170/7170-Volume3-0382/1588*? [accessed 19 June 2018].

238 UK Genealogy Archives, *Newport Pagnell, Buckinghamshire*. UK Genealogical Archives (n.d.). Transcribed from: *A Topographical Dictionary of England*, ed. Samuel Lewis, *British History Online* (London, 1848). *http://www.british-history.ac.uk/topographical-dict/england* [accessed 11 July 2020].

239 John Nichols, *The Progresses, Processions, and Magnificent Festivities, of King James the First*, vol. 2 (London, 1828).

240 Susan Dunn Hensley, *Anna of Denmark and Henrietta Maria: Virgins, Witches, and Catholic Queens* (Palgrave, 2017), p.99.

it seems quite possible they would have been acquainted with Anne's sister, were she present, Catherine Princess of Turley. Otherwise Catherine might have been a Cinderella figure or maybe a character disguised at the masque.

Queen Anne and King James' daughter was placed with Lady Harington. Anne's ladies-in-waiting included: Lucy Russell (b. Harington), Lady Bedford and her mother. There was the Countess of Derby also the Countess of Worcester; Lady Southwell and Lady Rich. Sadly in 1612, young and popular Prince Henry had only two years left, his death would cast his brother Charles into Henry's position as heir.

Robert was the last known Terhull, who died in the 1500s. His daughter Katherine married Thomas Persehouse and they lived at Turls Hill. In a survey of 1614, Edward Persehouse was living at Turls Hill, Woodsetton, and doing homage as a customary tenement. His daughter Anna married Thomas Gibbons in 1662. The early family probably lived in the Old Park Lodge. In the 16th century, the Park's family occupied Parkhouse Hall, then an impressive address. By the next century, the family held substantial lands in and around Sedgley. Their surname altered from Parks, which the Barons called them until the mid-1600s. After that the family used the place name Parkhouse, which morphed into Persehouse. By the 1700s, their mansion was Persehouse Hall, its demolition came in the 1800s when a reservoir was constructed.[241]

The Persehouse family (alt. Parkes, Pursehouse)

All Saints Church contains a memorial to Elizabeth, wife of Edward Parkhouse of Nether Gornal, plus other commemoration of Edward himself, this time with the more usual Persehouse spelling, the inscription on one of the four bells mentions "Peeter Parshous Esq." Descendants of these families would be churchwardens in 1720. Early volumes of the Parish Registers commencing 1558 contain an entry in the 17th century for Thomas Tomlinson, commonly called 'Dobbin', nicknames were often added to burials and remained common in the Dudley area for centuries.[242]

241 Dudley Metropolitan Borough Council, 'Township of Sedgley 1750', produced by John Hemingway and Jennifer Foster (Dudley, 2006), bibliog. col. map, pdf 57.24kb. *https://www.dudley.gov.uk/residents/planning/historic-environmenthistoric-maps-of-dudley/* [accessed 16 October 2020]. (Dudley's historic maps can be viewed from 1307 to the present day). 'Woodsetton Township'.

242 Percy Thoresby Jones, *The Story of All Saints Parish Church Sedgley* (1935). (Available from the church). Parish Records commencing 1558.

Many burial entries related to men "kild in the colepits", such as some that were killed by choke-damp like Andrew and Edward, unfortunate colliers in 1685. When people refer to Dudley people of those times as quaint, it could be partly due to a lilt in their speech, still around in the 1960s, for example 'plea-as' for please or 'Duderley' for Dudley. Is it an influence from Picardy or Wales? Birmingham people developed their speech from having been isolated because the area lacked navigable rivers. Whatever the reasons, Shakespeare would have had a Warwickshire accent similar to Birmingham's, but Dudley speech would have varied very much from both Birmingham and Wolverhampton's tongues, which both differed from each other anyway.

The saga tree also contains direct ancestor Hickmans ancestors. There were two All Saints vicars in 1625, Thomas Hickmans and William Pinner (D.D. Cantab), three years later the post went to William Parks (M.A. Cantab). Credentials after vicars' names are evidence of the emergence of a more highly educated clergy than earlier.

Dudley 25th Baron and Elizabeth Tomlinson's daughter Jane and Richard Thomas Persehouse would be grandparents to ironmaster Abraham Darby I. They married in 1609 at Tipton. Richard Thomas had been baptised in Sedgley in 1588 and died in 1626, the year a pew carving in his name was placed in All Saints Church. Incidentally, the original organ of All Saints came from Westminster Abbey.[243] Surely, this could only come about through contacts in high places? Richard had been Esquire to Sir Ferdinando at the Investiture of Prince Henry, in fact Ferdinando was made Knight of the Bath on 4 June 1610.[244] Richard too, perhaps, had known Catherine, Princess of Turley, had the Sutton Dudleys and the Persehouses mingled at Queen Anne's court. Before John Turley's marriage in 1600, he could have been in the company of Dudley people in London, in service at court, or in another capacity where he met Catherine. Richard Persehouse was an attorney there's a possibility that John Turley was a lawyer too.

From Dudley Archives it is known that Henry Jackson (Henricus Jacson vicarious) was appointed Vicar of St. Edmund's in 1609. He was amongst the wealthiest of Dudley townsmen and a signatory to Richard Barnes, Headmaster of Wolverhampton Grammar School, who refused to permit

243 Sedgley Local History Society, *Sedgley: Around the Manor: Sites and Scenes – Past and Present. http://www.Sedgleylocalhistory.org.uk* [accessed 6 July 2016].

244 Staffordshire, *Collections for a History of Staffordshire* (1888).

children of recusants into his school unless their parents allowed them to attend church. Henry Jackson liked and backed Barnes. Dudley Castle occupied an enclave within Worcestershire. In 1626, Henry Jackson's probate inventory at Worcester disclosed his mansion had seven main rooms and many chambers. The 'studie of bookes' was valued at £13 6s 8d. White meat in the kitchen was worth 10 shillings. His silver was listed under Plate, which few owned then. The entire estate was worth £103 4s 4d. An appraiser was Richard Foley, an influential entrepreneur, who owned furnaces, forges and slitting mills, of which his mill on the Stour at Kinver was the first to aid nail rod production.[245] Richard Foley, St. Thomas (Terrier) became the second Mayor of Dudley in 1615, the first was Humphrey Jukes, St. Thomas (Terrier). It was around 1610 that the Latin copy of a document in the Dudley Estate archives referred to the manors of Dudley being granted to "George Baggaley."[246] Chitham wrote that Ferdinando and Oliver Dixon were in charge of the coal works at Knowle Hill, Dudley.[247]

Edward Dudley 25th treated his children by Elizabeth Tomlinson very well. Their son Dodonis (Dud, b.1599/1600) probably spent his boyhood around Dudley Castle grounds. He appears to have been a favourite of the Earl's. From early childhood, the boy had shown enormous interest in mechanical pursuits, which his father had encouraged. Already, as a youth, Dud had been capable of increasing revenue for the earldom, using his skills with iron-making on behalf of the estate's furnaces and forges. Dud was at Balliol College aged 20. One furnace and two forges belonging to the Earl, especially works at Pensnett Chase, needed a trustworthy manager and so Dud agreed to return from Oxford to accept this responsibility when his father recalled him circa 1619.[248] He devised a method of smelting iron ore using coke at the baron's works in Cradley and Pensnett Chase but trading the idea proved harder to achieve.[249] It was a time when there was a shortage of charcoal. Deforestation of the countryside alarmed Parliamentarians.

---

245 Harold Parsons, *Portrait of the Black Country* (London, 1986), p.29.

246 Dudley Archives, Dudley Estate Archive, 'Manors of Dudley granted to George Baggeley' (17 February 8 Jas 1 1610-1611).

247 Edward Chitham, *The Story of Dudley* (Stroud, 2014), illus., p.76. Fn. 29 Court, pp.156-158.

248 Carl Higgs, *Sedgley Men of Iron: Dud Dudley and Abraham Darby – Keeping it in the Family!* Illus. *http://www.sedgleymanor.com/people/dud_dudley.html* [accessed 19 March 2016].

249 P.W. King, 'Dud Dudley's contribution to metallurgy', in *Hist. Metall.* (2002), vol. 22 (issue 1), pp.43-53.

Dud's inventive mind was ahead of them even though Staffordshire was not one of the worst affected counties.[250] The first patent was granted around 1620-1621 from James I to Lord Dudley, Dud's employer as well as father, so that Dud could carry on smelting iron.[251] Some believe that Edward obtained a licence to use the patent of John Robinson (or Rovenson) for making iron with pit-coal (mineral coal) in 1619, which he renewed in his own name in 1622. It's true that early patentees were Rovenzon and others from abroad, which were recorded in a *Great Seal* at the Patent Office. However, Patent number 117 of the Old Series was not granted until 1638 when it went to Sir George Horsey, David Ramsay, Roger Foulke and Dud Dudley.[252] [253]

Sir Ferdinando Dudley

Heir to Edward Sutton Dudley 25th's estates, Sir Ferdinando Dudley (married to Honora Seymour, daughter of Edward Seymour) died in his early 30s in 1621, predeceasing his father. Consequently the Baron's inheritance went to Frances (1611-1697), Fernando's daughter by Honora. Edward Seymour was styled Viscount Beauchamp and Honora had been considered by some to be a potential claimant to the throne when Elizabeth I died.

Dudley town

Dudley town was a mildly conservative place, influenced by ironstone families. Catholicism persisted in most towns whereas literate people, used to running guilds from generations back, tended to adopt the intellectual appeal of urban Protestantism, which was:

> "independence rather than belonging to a large body; freedoms from Elizabethan church dogma."

---

250 John Alfred Langford, et al., 'The Rise and Progress of the Manufacturers of Staffordshire' in *Staffordshire and Warwickshire Past and Present* (London and Birmingham, printed 1884), vol. 1., pp.xxvii-xxxii, illus. from original drawings by H. Warren.

251 Carl Higgs, *Sedgley Men of Iron: Dud Dudley and Abraham Darby – Keeping it in the Family!*

252 Samuel Smiles, *Industrial Biography, Iron Workers and Tool Makers*, 'Iron-smelting by Pit-coal Dud Dudley' from the 1863 ed. [Orig. published 1889, available from Heperides Press] (2006). Dud Dudley, *Metallum Martis* (1665). *Great Seal,* Patent Office, reprint (1858). Patent Office, Patent no. 117, granted to Sir George Horsey, David Ramsay, Roger Foulke and Dud Dudley. *http://www.lostlabours.co.uk/agenoria/research/duddud.htm* [also accessed 20 July 2020].

253 P.W. King, 'Dud Dudley's contribution to metallurgy', *Hist. Metall.* (2002), 22(1), pp.43-53.

Both had been constant factors earlier.

Dud Dudley

Prejudices and jealousies from charcoal burning iron smelters thwarted everything Dud tried to do because his new process using pit-coal was superior to theirs. During James I's reign, Dud's endeavours went badly:

> "A long remembered great 'May-Day flood' hit his Cradley works in 1623; He was accused of 'dangerous innovation'; Lies were told to the king that Dud's iron was unmerchantable."

Dud was no dud, he could make better iron at a cheaper rate than his competitors and the ironmasters and ironmongers were silenced for a time but further persecution against him recommenced in 1624:

> "Competitors succeeded in limiting Dud's patent from 31 to 14 years; Dud's patent was included in a list of abolished monopolies."

By the 21st year of James I's reign, Richard Parkshouse of Sedgley was Dud Dudley's brother-in-law. Dud made it known that Richard favoured his invention and:

> "had a fowling gun there made of pit-cole iron, which was well approved."

The authorities had indeed called it, "good merchantable iron."

Pathetic attempts at stopping Dud clearly indicated widespread fear of old methods being overtaken by new, these were typical misbehaviours against unwelcome progress. Dud himself stayed above it all and was variously described as: patient, undaunted, capable of greater ardour than before, cheerful in carrying on; and even Phoenix-like when malicious competitors resorted to filing lawsuits against him, aimed at ousting him from the Cradley Works. Dud could be relied upon to bounce back.

He successfully sold iron for £12 per ton to diverse customers and produced cast-iron wares such as cisterns, pots, mortars and more, knowing that these products were better as well as cheaper than any previously made with charcoal in Britain. The reason he could be described as 'rising from ashes' came because without Cradley yet again he had to resort to Himley. There his problem was having a furnace without a forge. Then he was forced to sell his pig iron to the charcoal ironmasters, who still tried to undermine him by detaining his stock and disparaging his iron.

What did Dud, the real iron man, do? Hasco Bridge, also known as Askew Bridge, is near Sedgley on the border between Gornal and Himley. It was on the old turnpike road from Dudley to Wellington. Dud moved there and erected "a furnace of stone, 27 feet square, with very large bellows" able to turn out seven tons of iron per week:

> "the greatest quantity of pit-coal iron ever yet made in Great Britain".

Dud's own words.

Of course, the new coke-fired furnace built at Hasco Bridge was accompanied by an unwelcome assault from Dud's enemies:

> "A riotous mob instigated by charcoal ironmasters invaded his premises;
> Dud's bellows were cut to pieces; Machinery was broken down;
> Dud's manufactures faced ruination."

With his furnace sabotaged, Dud was evicted. Lawsuits followed which plunged him into debt and caused his imprisonment for "seven thousand pounds". Better than for seven years but he described the experience as months in "duration vile."[254]

In St. Thomas, Dudley, *Churchwardens Book* 1618-1725/6 p.66, a poor levy was charged to Edward Bagly of 1s and Dudley Baggly the same amount.[255] On 10 April 1625 a conveyance of the mortgage of Himley Manor and other lands, specified transfers from Baron Edward Sutton to George Bagley/Thomas Parks to Sir William Cockayne.[256] Churchwardens assigned people to the Protestant pews that replaced plain benches. Sermons were so much longer than before, perhaps two slow hours, so long that 'pew rage' violence sometimes broke out. Despite such social reactions, and although

254 John Alfred Langford, et al., 'The Rise and Progress of the Manufacturers of Staffordshire'.

255 Dudley, *St. Thomas's Churchwardens Book* 1618-1725/6, p.66.

256 Dudley Archives and Local History Service, 'Conveyance of the Mortgage of the Manor at Himley and other lands' (10 April 1625).

conversion was a slow process, congregations changed gradually as new ways became more familiar.

During James I's reign he had angered many Scots through trying to force the Church of Scotland into English church ways and expecting bishops to obey. The concept of the Divine Right of Kings allowed him to believe his authority came straight from God without question while Protestant reformers like John Knox preferred the alternative Presbyterian views of John Calvin. Parliament had not been allowed to challenge James. Trade barriers between England and Scotland actually fared well under his reign as did legal reform and the justice system. The King died in 1625, succeeded by his son Charles.

Charles I – reigned 1625-1649

Dud Dudley petitioned the new King to renew his licence and with the help of three capitalists, Dud did what Dud did, he carried on iron-making. Only the outbreak of Civil War would eventually stop him. A jury of 1641 chose two men to be constables, one was a Richard Parkes. Another jury (for the foreign) was held on 21 October 1641, a Richard Parkes sat on that board too. It seems he was a busy man. Foreigners were relatives or servants (also known as 'inmates'), who came to live with Dudley householders. Their arising health needs became problematic. Other *Churchwardens' Book* entries refer to Sutton Bagley with his kinsman Jevon Harper in the role of overseers in March 1695.[257] Taplin spoke of Sutton Bagley being a churchwarden in 1696, most probably John and Olive's child (b.1637).

Cover of Metallum Martis by Dud Dudley (1665, reprint), photograph from the Cox collection.

257 Dudley, St. Thomas, *Churchwardens' Book*, 1618-1725/6, pp.244, 246.

Memorials

Dud Dudley married Eleanor Heaton (1606-1675) on 12 October 1626.[258] Dud set up a lasting memorial to her in St. Helen's, Worcester. He may have remarried.[259]

A carved pew back remains at All Saints, Sedgley, in Richard Persehouse's name:

RICAY DVS PARRSHOUSE DE HO

The pew back was not in situ but stacked ahead of the left-side front row near the font, giving the following information:

> "This early 17th century pew back survives from the original All Saints', rebuilt in 1829. It was built by Richard Parkshouse of Holly Hill, Ettingshall, in 1626. Richard was an attorney who married Jane, the natural daughter of Lord Dudley, making him brother-in-law to Dud Dudley. He was involved with Dud's exploits in the early use of coal to smelt iron, by transporting samples to the Tower of London for testing. His daughter Margaret, married John Darby, ancestor of the Coalbrookdale Darbys."

On 10 December 1649, Edward (alt. Parkhouse) probably acted as attorney for a lease transaction between John 'Darbye' locksmith and Baron Humble Ward. Edward was brother of John Darby's wife Margaret and these siblings were nephew and niece to Dud Dudley.[260] Seven years later, John of Sedgley and Margaret Darby's children were accepted into Dudley Friends' Meeting House. Edward married Mary Cooper at the Meeting House in 1671.

There used to be two inscribed ironwork gates described as tablets inside All Saints, one in memory of Richard and Jane's eldest son, Edward (1608-1685), the other in memory of his second wife. A wall mounted memorial remains:

---

258 Dud Dudley, *Metallum Martis* 1st pub. 1665, 2nd ed, by John N. Bagnall (December 1854). As cited by Dud Dudley: Included Reproduction works of Rovenson and Simo Sturtevant, 1612/1613. 'The Publisher to the Reader' mentions W. Baldwin, Esq. of Ellowes, Sedgley, (December 1854). Subscribers (to the 2nd ed.) included E. Elwell, Esq., Wednesbury Forge.

259 Carl Higgs, *Sedgley Men of Iron: Dud Dudley and Abraham Darby – Keeping it in the Family!*

260 Carl Higgs, *Sedgley Men of Iron: Dud Dudley and Abraham Darby – Keeping it in the Family!*

> "In memory of Edward Persehouse of Lower Gornal who here lyeth interred betwixt his two wives Elizabeth daughter of Thomas Bradley of the Wood in this Parish. Gen his first wife and Margaret daughter to John Asteley of Bushbury in this County [Staffordshire]. Gen his second wife. He entered into rest May the 13th Ano Dni Deum Anog. Aetat suqe 75 Foelix mutation ubi Deum pro mundo accepimus pro terrena Coelestia."

Lower Gornal was one of the nine villages comprising Sedgley. Edward was a lawyer and Staffordshire coroner, his wives Margaret and Elizabeth Persehouse should not be confused with Margaret and Elizabeth Persehouse, daughters of Richard Persehouse of Sedgley (d.1656) and granddaughters of Jane Sutton Dudley.

Although Edward Sutton Dudley 25th outlived his legitimate heir Ferdinando, in 1628 he had managed to arrange a lucrative marriage in 1628 for his granddaughter Frances to Sir Humble Ward (b.1614), only son and heir to William Ward of Cheapside, a London goldsmith, who would be jeweller to the court of Charles I.[261] Humble was one of Edward's creditors, the last of the Sutton Dudley barons.[262] William Ward's wife was Elizabeth (with connections to Southwark).

At some point, Dud's father gave him the lease of Chasepool Lodge, Swindon in Staffordshire. Although he was promised the manor of Himley and probably spent time there, he never received it. He and his father had a quarrel, which seems to have concerned a misunderstanding about his entitlement to Himley. The hall eventually passed legally to the Ward family; a matter discussed by Higgs, citing Rollason and also Radmore.[263]

Sedgley Manor, with its appurtenances, including rectorial tithes and advowson, was held from 1600-1672 by the Parkes family. It had passed to them by purchase and was returned to the Wards through the marriage of Anne Parkes to Humble and Ward's son William. Thomas Parkes lived at Willingsworth Hall, half a mile from Wednesbury.

---

261 Dudley Council, *History of Himley Hall*, handout.

262 Cracroft's Peerage: The Complete Guide to the British Peerage & Baronetage, Ward, Baron (E, 1643/4), Heraldic Media Limited (London).

263 Carl Higgs, *Sedgley Men of Iron: Dud Dudley and Abraham Darby – Keeping it in the Family!* Fn. 24 A.A. Rollason, 'The seamy side of Dud Dudley and his father'. Also David F. Radmore, 'Himley Hall & Park – A History'.

Elizabeth Tomlinson's Will

Elizabeth Tomlinson had died in 1629, the date of her nuncupative (oral) will. Higgs states that Edward and his brother Dudley were both nephews of Elizabeth, being sons of John Bagley (1572-1648) and as such Edward administered Elizabeth's estate in 1635. Three years later, the 1638 jury, whose number included Baron Edward Sutton Dudley, had examined a very significant legacy from Elizabeth, she had left £40-£50, a debt owed to her. The money was to benefit the poor. Executors, appointed at her death, said they would sell a horse to raise the money but apparently had not done so nine years later because the horse still belonged to executor Thomas Dudley. If money had been raised another way, it had not been paid to the poor.[264] How disappointing that Thomas Dudley let her down as executor of her will.

Consulting *Index to the Prerogative Court of Canterbury*, Colonel Hansen found the following record concerning Elizabeth's will:

> "Eliz. Spin. [Spinster] Tipton, Staffs to Edw. BAGLEY, neph. Ex sis 19 June 1637, p.107, revealing that Edward Bagley was the administrator of Elizabeth Tomlinson's nuncupative will, describing him as 'fill…'. This word was struck out and overwritten with the words 'nepoti' ex maternal nephew, or simply relative."

Hansen's research seems to have been undertaken in search of William Brinton's ancestral link to US President Richard Nixon.[265] William and Ann Brinton emigrated to Philadelphia circa 1684. They were descendants of Ann Tomlinson (Elizabeth's sister) and John Bagley (1572-1648). From Dudley Archives it is known that John Bagley was buried on 15 May 1648 at St. Thomas, Dudley.[266] John's own will informed Taplin that John was a yeoman in the service of Lord Dudley, a warden or estate manager and, at a later time,

---

264 Edward Chitham, *The Story of Dudley*.

265 John Taplin, *Shakespeare's Granddaughter and the Bagleys of Dudley; an investigation of their relationship and that of others to the last direct descendant of William Shakespeare* (n.d.). *https://blackcountrysociety.co.uk/articles/bagley.htm* [accessed 30 March 2016]. William Brinton, (Brinton family link to US President Richard Nixon). *http://www.brintonfamily.org* Charles M. Hansen, 'The Ancestry of William and Ann Brinton', *The American Genealogist. http://www.brintonfamily.org* Marc Fitch, Index to the Prerogative Court of Canterbury (1988), p.416.

266 Dudley Archives, St. Thomas's, 15 May 1648, John Bagley's burial.

a leaseholder of the Earl's deer park (1611) and rabbit warren (connigree) at Old Park[267]. British History Online (BHO) refers to estates belonging to Baron Dudley going to George Baggeley, yeoman.[268]

Persehouse line

Thomas Persehouse, John Persehouse, Richard Persehouse, Adam Persehouse and other named people were notional owners of 'Our Lady's Lands' granted to Cecilia Pickerell as payment for a debt by the Duke of Northumberland (Lord Sutton). These lands comprised 14 properties. The rents from the properties were to be used to establish a school and for other charitable purposes. It is unknown how much of the money that should have been put in trust materialised because there was a malfunction. Back in 1562, the intention had been to fund a grammar school. In September 1638 an inquisition by jury took place, involving prominent aristocrats including Edward Dudley 25th Baron, to find out what had gone wrong. The descendants of the original 1562 trustees were questioned. Many had not paid the rents for the maintenance of the school. John and Thomas Persehouse held land in Stoney Lane and had paid their rents due to the manor. It turned out that the Mayor and bailiffs had misused the payments in 1562. Richard Persehouse (1500-1540) married Agnes, their son was Thomas Persehouse (b.1520) therefore he could have been present in 1562. Richard Persehouse (Parkes, 1613-1656) could have been present in 1638, son of direct ancestors of Jane Dudley and Richard of the pew, direct ancestors, whose grandson was Thomas Persehouse born in Nether Gornal, Sedgley in 1669. The outcome of the meeting was the appointment of a new group of trustees to be led by Richard Foley.

The Bagley family

The baptism records for Bagley descendants show the name Edward Bagley was common to both generations. Of two Edward Bagleys, scholars had concentrated on the one whose mother's name was Mary and overlooked

---

267 John Taplin, *Shakespeare's Granddaughter and the Bagleys of Dudley.*

268 BHO, 'Parishes: Dudley' in *A History of the County of Worcester: vol. 3.* (London: orig. published by Victoria County History, 1913), pp.90-105. Fn. 95 Available on privacy page in 1612 the revision and remainders depending upon the estates in fee tail belonging to Lord Dudley were granted to a certain George Baggaley, yeoman (Parti Jas I, pt.xiii). *http://www.british-history.ac.uk/privacy* [accessed 30 March 2016].

the one whose mother's name was Olive. Taplin combined Bagley data with genealogies in three very interesting articles published in *The Blackcountryman* articles.[269] The following tables resulted:

Table 1 – Baptisms in Dudley of John and Mary Bagley's children, **John Taplin, *Shakespeare's Granddaughter and the Bagleys of Dudley.***	
Edward Bagley*	18 Oct. 1602, St. Edmund
John Bagley	29 Dec. 1603, St. Edmund
Dudley Bagley	1 Sep. 1605, St. Edmund
Unnamed Daughter	27 Dec. 1606, St. Thomas
Elyzabeth	9 Feb. 1607/8, St. Thomas
Thomas	May 1610, St. Thomas
Robart	12 Sep. 1612, St. Edmund
Richard	29 July 1616, Sedgley
*Edward the eldest married Olive.	

Table 2 – Baptisms in Dudley of Edward and Ann Olive Bagley's children, **John Taplin, *Shakespeare's Granddaughter and the Bagleys of Dudley.***	
Ann Bagley	27 April 1634, St. Edmund
Suttons Bagley	22 April 1637, St. Thomas
Edward Bagley	6 June 1641, St. Thomas
John Bagley	14 April 1644, St. Edmund

Shakespearean researchers were interested in Edward Bagley, who was connected to the last direct descendant of Shakespeare's granddaughter Dame Elizabeth Barnard (alt. Bernard, b. Hall, d. 16 Feb. 1670, buried St. Peter's, Abingdon). In 1626, she had married her first husband Thomas Nash, who died 1647. Two years later she married Sir John Barnard.

Baldwin Bernard of Abington had a sister named Anne D'Oyley or Doyley. In 1601, Sir James Harington had married his only wife, Anne, who was John Doyley's wealthy widow. Anne's maiden name was Bernard. Theodosia Sutton Dudley (b. Harington) immediately springs to mind. The northern Haringtons owned land as far apart as Ireland and the English Midlands.

269 John Taplin, *Shakespeare's Granddaughter and the Bagleys of Dudley*, *The Blackcountryman*, Issues 38/4, 39/1 and 39/2, illus.

Taplin realised a different Edward Bagley of Dudley was key and not the one Shakespearean scholars had previously believed to be connected to William Shakespeare's last direct descendant, his granddaughter Elizabeth Hall.[270] Also, he speculated that Edward Bagley, son of Olive Bagley, could have been Lady or Dame Elizabeth Bernard's ward. An Edward Bagley had been named as executor and major beneficiary in the will of Elizabeth Bernard. The trustees of her will were Henry Smyth (or Smith) and Job Dighton. Their task was to sell off all of her estate, including Nash's house in Chapel Street, Stratford-upon-Avon, adjacent to New Place. As decreed to happen, Thomas Nash's cousin Edward Nash received first refusal on the part of the estate not otherwise bequeathed after her second husband's death in 1674. If declined, the trustees were told to pass this part of the inheritance to Edward Bagley, her "loving kinsman." She made Edward Bagley her only executor in 1675, calling him "a Citizen and Pewterer of London." The point relevant to Dudley 25th Baron's wife and mistress is that Edward Bagley, Pewterer, was a direct descendant of Elizabeth Tomlinson's sister Anne. Also, Theodosia was aunt to Baldwin Bernard's son, Sir John Bernard.

Archivists of Shakespeare Birthplace Trust, Stratford-upon-Avon, found records (ref ER2/BF) for Edward Bagley's apprenticeship with the Pewterers' Company [of London]:

> "12 September 1656: Robert Orme presented Edward Dudley, son of Edward deceased, of Dudley in Staffordshire, gentleman, for 8 years from All Saints Day – 2s.
>
> 6 October 1664: Edward Bagley, apprentice to Robert Orme sworne and made free 6s 8d."

Elizabeth and Anne Tomlinson's mother had the surname Orre, similar in this context to Orme as name alternatives were so common. The Great Orme is on the North Wales coast near Anglesey of course. The apprenticeship date would make Edward an appropriate age, i.e. 15 years old in 1656. This Edward was Elizabeth Tomlinson's great-nephew, young Edward's mother's name was Olive not Mary.

270 John Taplin, *Shakespeare's Granddaughter and the Bagleys of Dudley, The Blackcountryman, Issues* 38/4, 39/1 and 39/2, illus. Shakespeare Birthplace Trust, Records Office, Papers of Richard Savage, file ref. ER82/11/6/1.

Taplin also referred to Shakespeare Birthplace Trust records:

> "This person (who it is believed, was not related to Shakespeare, but kinsman either of Sir John Barnard or to the family of Hall or Nash) must have become possessed of all her Coffers & Cabinets in which undoubtedly were several of her gfathers papers. When & where Mr Bagley died, is uncertain, no will of his having been discovered in the Prerof Office tho' the search has been made for 50 yrs. Suseqt. To 1670."

John Taplin's argument is convincing but goodness knows where Dame Elizabeth's missing coffers and cabinets went or what they contained.

Chitham provided a glimpse of the lives of Bagleys locally, identifying John Bagley as one of the Dudley borough jurors, who was told to build a fence in Peacocks Field by the jury for the 'foreign' held 21 October 1641. In 1642, the borough court roll asked George Bagley to scour the ditch leading from his barn to Woddam's Hill (outside the actual borough). Sam Bagley had houses at Wadams Hill and Richard Bagley's family were in Hall Street, and were evaluated for levy in 1649.[271]

The English Civil War

Nationally the English Long Parliament, summoned by Charles I, had sat from November 1640.

Battle of Edgehill, 23 October 1642

Charles I declared war on his Long Parliament and its supporters in August because all attempts at constitutional compromises between Oliver Cromwell and the King had failed. This was the first battle of the English Civil War it took place in South Warwickshire near Banbury with Robert Devereux in command, 3rd Earl of Essex. Charles' nephew, Bohemian born Prince Rupert of the Palatine (1619-1682) was with the Royalists. He was the son of Frederick V, Elector of the Palatine, and Elizabeth, 'The White Queen', sister to Charles, and had grown up in the court of the Prince of Orange in Holland.[272]

---

271 Edward Chitham, *The Story of Dudley*, pp.62-63.

272 BCW Project, British Civil Wars, Commonwealth & Protectorate 1638-1660. *Prince Rupert of the Rhine, 1619-1682; King Charles' nephew and commander of the Royalist cavalry, https://bcw-project.com* [accessed 22 July 2020].

Edgehill was not a decisive battle against the Roundheads. The Earl of Clarendon wrote:[273]

> "At Edgehill… the foot soldiers stood their ground with great courage; and though many of the King's soldiers were unarmed and had only cudgels, they kept their ranks, and took up the arms which their slaughtered neighbours left to them."

Charles was discouraged from marching in good time to Shrewsbury from London, which proved a bad decision. Rupert was active in the Midlands in early 1643. Urban areas mostly comprised Parliamentarians whereas landowners and aristocrats sought control of rural areas and followed Charles. There was serious religious divide between Nonconformist townsfolk and traditional county loyalists.

Margaret Sutton Dudley's partner John Darby, a yeoman farmer, as well as a small mineral worker was possibly on Cromwell's side in the Civil War, the Darbys were Quakers from John's time.

Newport Pagnell, 1643

Newport Pagnell was taken by the Earl of Essex. The same year in March, the English Long Parliament ended. Summoned by Charles I in November 1640, it had continued through the English Civil War to this point and would be restored for a short time in 1659 before going forward into the subsequent interregnum and final vote for its own dissolution in 1660.

Death of Edward, last Sutton Baron and Dudley 25th Baron

Edward died, probably intestate, on 23 June 1643 and was buried at St. Edmunds, Dudley.[274] As 25th Baron, he was succeeded by Sir Humble, 1st Baron Ward and his wife Frances, Edward and Theodosia's granddaughter, Baroness Dudley *suo jure*. In his new capacity, Humble paid debts and redeemed estates for the benefit of himself, Frances and their descendants.

---

273 John Simkin, *Edward Hyde, Earl of Clarendon* [b.1609 Salisbury, 1674], British-History, The English Civil [online]. War (1997, updated January 2020). *john@spartacus-educational.com* [accessed 10 September 2020]. Earl of Clarendon, *The History of the Rebellion* (1667).

274 *History of Parliament: the House of Commons 1558-1603*, ed. P.W. Hasler (1981). *http://www.historyofparliamentonline.org/volume/1558-1603/* [accessed 15 October 2017].

Although the 24th and 25th Sutton Dudley Barons were ironmasters plagued by serious debts, through their coalfields, mineral and ore sources in Dudley they were early enablers of the Industrial Revolution.

Aston Hall Attack, December 1643

Sir Thomas Holte was visited by Charles I in August 1642 as the King made his way south from Shrewsbury where he had raised troops prior to Edgehill. When Jacobean Aston Hall was threatened with attack, Sir Thomas sought help from the Dudleys. Royalist soldiers were sent from the garrison at Dudley Castle to protect the mansion and defensive earthworks were quickly created in the park. When the siege came, the interior staircase banister was damaged by a cannonball which was probably shot through a drawing room to the left of the stairs. Forty musketeers defended Holte's home but surrendered after three days of bombardment.[275]

Bolton Massacre (Storming of Bolton), 28 May 1644

Leading to the Civil War, the county of Lancashire was particularly tense as social and economic changes increased. Calvinism was prevalent in Bolton, causing the town to be called the 'Geneva of the North'. James Stanley (1607-1651), 7th Earl of Derby, was a prominent figure in Lancashire; he fought at the Bolton Massacre as well as in the Battle of Marston Moor and elsewhere on the Royalists' side.[276] Bolton was mindlessly plundered with disregard for civilian lives. Stanley was known during his lifetime as Lord Strange. The story of Barons' Strange was indeed strange, having four separate creations: in 1295, 1299, 1326 and 1628. The latter was applied by error to this 7th Earl. The Derby family seat is Knowsley Hall, named from the historic hundred of (West Derby) in South Lancashire.

Dudley Castle, 1st Siege and Skirmish, Tipton Green, June 1644

Dudley Castle was garrisoned by royalist troops and besieged twice. This first attempt by the Earl of Denbigh was unsuccessful although Dudley Castle suffered some damage that was remedied. Tipton Green's siege and skirmish

275 Birmingham City Council, Birmingham Museums, *Aston Hall* (n.d.). https:// *www.birminghammuseums.org.uk* [accessed 19 October 2017].

276 Lancashire Archives, *Stanley Family Collection*, DDF 985 1015, 2420-2422, 2431. *https://archives.lancashire.gov.uk* [accessed 9 September 2020].

were two chaotic events covered in great detail by Hemingway.[277] Kinsman of Dudley barons, another Edward Dudley, had his mansion on the Green targeted by musketeers at the beginning.

Sir William Brereton had his sights on Dudley Castle yet his prime objective was Lichfield Close.

Battle of Marston Moor, 2 July 1644, evening

This was the first major royal defeat. The combined forces of the English Parliament under Sir Thomas, 3rd Baron Fairfax, the Earl of Manchester and Scottish Covenanters under the Earl of Leven defeated the Royalists commanded by Prince Rupert and the Marquess of Newcastle.

Battle of Naseby, 14 June 1645

Charles I encamped in the grounds of Himley Hall, near Dudley, on his way to the Battle of Naseby, which was fought 20 miles south of Leicester. Naseby was the last and most vital battle of the First Civil War (1642-1645). It was a definite Parliamentarian victory by a reformed New Model Army under Fairfax and Oliver Cromwell against King Charles with Prince Rupert. Rupert had captured Leicester but lost Naseby that foggy morning, outnumbered two to one by Parliamentarians.

The second attempt against Dudley Castle was by Sir William Brereton, a Parliamentary General. The royalist garrison was under the command of Colonel Thomas Leveson and included an attack on the nearby Priory.

Newport Pagnell, 1645

Sir Samuel Luke garrisoned the town.

Dudley, last siege, 1646
Excerpts from letters between Sir Thomas Leveson and Sir William Brereton:

123. General's order upon Intelligence out of Lichfield Close, 28 April 1646, Dudley. (Having sent some forces thither to besiege Dudley Castle) Sir

---

277 John Hemingway, *An Illustrated Chronicle of the Castle and Barony of Dudley 1070-1757* (Dudley, 2006), pp.95-109, b. & w. and col. illus., map.

William Brereton sent strict orders to... Col. Jackson and Mr Broughton on the city side to be very vigilant and watchful and to send out a party of firelocks to discover the enemy's works...

(Colonel Philip Jackson of Stanshope in Alstonfield, Staffordshire (d.1675), a prominent member of the Staffordshire committee and a moderate opponent of Brereton's control. He was probably the so-called 'Grand juryman' reported in London as instrumental in raising the Moorlanders in 1643.)

125. Thomas Leveson to Brereton, 28 April 1646, Dudley Castle: Beaumont's wife being dead, I shall take it for a favour if you will permit us to bury her in the upper church of Dudley without interruption. (p.104)

127. Brereton to Thomas Leveson, 28 April 1646, Dudley: ... to bury Lt.-Col. Beaumont's wife in the upper church, which is such a civility as I will not deny... some of my soldiers... were shot by your men contrary to the law... If you send the names of such as shall accompany her interment, you shall receive a pass for them. (p.105)

128. Thomas Leveson to Brereton, 28 April 1646, Dudley Castle: ... For your men that were shot coming to receive my drum it was contrary to my orders nor do I know by whom 'twas done... you will find I am not to be frighted from my resolution... that for which concerns the King's service I wish with all my heart your guilt were no greater than [mine]. (p.110)

138. Col. Leveson to Brereton, 29 April 1646, Dudley Castle: ... I have prisoners here... Edward Crew belonging to Capt. Hill at the garrison of Chepstow, whom I am willing to release for Ensign Capelwood taken by the country men about Kinver on Saturday last at night. (p.138)[278]

278 Staffordshire, *Collections for a History of Staffordshire*, 'The Civil War in Staffordshire in the Spring of 1646: Sir William Brereton's Letter Book, April-May 1646', ed. Ivor Carr and Ian Atherton (2007), vol. 21 (Fourth Series). J. Parkes, *A History of Tipton* (Tipton, 1915), pp.201-202. (Ensign William Capplewood of Leveson's foot claimed as an indigent officer from Staffordshire. He was possibly the man of this name who signed the protestation at Tipton in March 1642. *List*. Col. 84). Staffs. Historical Collection(3), Dore, ii, 721. (Fourth series), ii, p.20.

139. Col. Leveson to Brereton, 29 April 1646, Dudley Castle: I have sent unto you those three prisoners I mentioned and shall desire my ensign may be sent tomorrow… (p.141)

140. Brereton to Col. Leveson, 29 April 1646, Dudley: The prisoners you mention are all unknown to me yet because you were pleased upon my desire to release Edward Ensor I will send you Ensign Capelwood according to your desire… Capelwood… was intended to have been executed by the same justice that you executed Hamilton… (p.119)

150. Brereton to Colonel Leveson, 30 April 1646, Dudley: …hereafter I shall take it for no courtesy to send me… desire not exchange… [Post] Two… are so extremely wounded that they were carried down upon barrows and no better than dead men as I have been informed… (pp.141-142)

169. Brereton to Col. Leveson, 6 May 1646, Dudley: …You cannot but be sufficiently informed of the King's present condition… therefore I shall not think fit to admit any further delay but do hereby require you in the name of both Houses of Parliament to deliver up the castle with all the arms, ammunition and other warlike provisions therein to me for the use of the King and Parliament… At nine of the clock tomorrow morning I expect your positive answer. (p.147)

179. Col. Leveson to Brereton, 7 May 1646, Dudley Castle: If you will be pleased to send me a pass by my drummer for the safe passage to you and return back of Lt. Col. Beaumont and Major Christopher Heveningham you shall by them receive an answer to your summons. (p.155)

180. Brereton to Col. Leveson, 7 May 1646, Dudley: I have according to your desire sent here enclosed a pass for Lt-Col. Beaumont and Major Heveningham whose coming forth accordingly is expected. (p.155)

181. *The pass* 7, May 1646, Dudley: To all colonels and inferior officers and soldiers belonging to this leaguer and to all others to whom it may come and concern in the Parliament's service. These are to require you and everyone of you upon sight hereof to permit Lt-Col. Beaumont and Major Heveningham

to pass this day from the castle of Dudley to me to my quarter in Dudley town and thence to return unto the said castle without any manner of violence or interruption. (p.156)[279]

Colonel Leveson surrendered the castle on behalf of his 340 men. Colonel Leveson's command had included an attack on the priory nearby. Defeat at the battle of Naseby and the imprisonment of the King left royalists without options.

Most interesting of all to this saga tree is the letter sent from Richard Pershouse a week after the surrender, suggesting that the gentry supported the King but did not seem to like Thomas Leveson. He had seen the Colonel galloping away,

> "with manie thousand curses of the cuntrie people, whoe would certainly have kil'd him had hee not beene strongly guarded with 2 troops of horse of the Parliament… he served the king a little, but himself most." [280]

Saint Edmund's Church, Dudley

St. Edmund's Church in Dudley had been destroyed, it was pulled down deliberately for strategic reasons. A 'My Lord' letter, dated 26 October 1646, concerned a delay in demolishing the castle:

> "expect your speedie answer."

Signatures were from "Your loving friends and servants." Local memorials of aristocrats were not normally smashed because it was understood how much they helped keep a community together. Interesting in 2020 debates about appropriate commemorations.

At least three antiquarians confirmed that the tomb of John VI Sutton 1st Dudley 20th (1400-1487) had been moved from the abandoned Priory Church to St. Edmund's, which had an effigy decorated with the Order of the Garter that was almost certainly destroyed in the 17th century along with St. Edmund's. His son William Dudley (b.1431) was kneeling before Our Lady marking his role of Bishop of Durham: a scroll coming from his mouth. It is not clear who was responsible for rebuilding this chapel (*huius capille*)

---

279 Staffordshire, *Collections for a History of Staffordshire.*

280 John Hemingway, *An Illustrated Chronicle of the Castle and Barony of Dudley 1070-1757.* p.109 Fn. 232 Johnson & Oiney, p.69, 5.0, D260/M/F/1/6, f8.

and organising the window placement. Doubt remains due to the existence of another Dudley chantry chapel.

The Dudley Castle siege had caused devastation. Later in the 1600s, John Parkes along with Jonathan Taylor reported that St. Edmund's Church was in good repair and that parishioners "diligently frequent the church." They did – to take materials from the rubble of St. Edmunds, their local outlet for sourcing new home building materials. Taylor and Parkes seem to have been trying to persuade the diocese that a new vicarage was needed. Church repairs continued but the diocese did not supply a new vicarage.

One of the Parkhouses, a market stallholder in the early 1700s, seemed not to have fared so well. Along with Bancester and Pinly, he was told to clear up better at the end of market day. Once they had taken down and removed their stalls, they were to attend to the "chanell by ye towne hall." In August 1703, widow Parkes of Windmill Hill defaulted on paying her required church levies. Richard Parkes of the Lodge (Netherton) did likewise. These Netherton residents are likely to have defaulted deliberately as the parish church on the hill (St. Thomas's) would have seemed remote to their lives.

In 1703, John Parkes of the Holt in Halesowen benefited from the will of Samuel Taylor, who owned land in Tansley Hill, near Dixon's Green. It was for the purpose of buying a house "fit for a School House and a School Master." The house purchased was in the lane that later became Stafford Street. Samuel Taylor was interested in giving poor boys the chance to learn to read, write and cast accounts. An extensive rare inventory of Netherton Hall Estate is contained in a marriage settlement document between Anne Holt, eldest daughter of Clobury Holte, and North Foley, whose grandfather was Lord North.[281] This was drawn up with the agreement of the heir to Aston, Clobury Holte. Aston Hall is ten miles from Netherton Hall. A different Richard Parkes also died in 1726, he was identified at the time of an undated Dudley Plan to be the owner of land from the will of Jonathan Taylor dated 1720. The plan was created between 1720 and 1726.

Lichfield Cathedral

The Civil War in Lichfield severely damaged one of the cathedral's three spires. Lichfield Close gardens leading to the cathedral were in danger of

---

281 Edward Chitham, *The Story of Dudley*, p.91.

being trampled underfoot during the fighting. Troops helped themselves to fruit and vegetables to eat wherever they went as kitchen gardens and orchards supplied sustenance. Legend says that High Arcal was a look-out post for the Dudley Castle garrison during the Civil War. In medieval times, Flaxhall, Woodsetton in Sedgley belonged to the Baron of Dudley and was the main farmstead (later called High Arcal). The Flaxhall family held the estate and served the lordship in rider (messenger) capacity. Walter de Flaxale paid tax of 5/6d in 1355. When Henry Hodgetts was dying in 1651, he told the Roman Catholic priest that he had the bones of St. Chad, brought from Lichfield Cathedral at the time of the Dissolution in the 1530s. Henry's wife gave the relics to Father Peter Turner. Eventually they reached the new cathedral of St. Chad's in Birmingham in 1933.[282]

From the Letter Book of Sir William Brereton[283]

159. Mr John Hill to 'his wife in the Fryers', 4 May 1646, Lichfield Close.

> "... the rest of the things you mention in the letter I have received and somewhat else 'the Tulyis' etc.* The plague or any other disease within us is not, about us it maybe. I am and so have been since my hither coming in as good health as ever... the heat of the weather will make me cautious in taking much tobacco."

It's hard to know what 'the Tulyis' could be, tiles, a unit or a family? Obviously the name Turley comes to mind but only because of its relevance to this family saga plus the mention of Stourbridge, which lies in the direction of Dudley. The 1700s saw history return to Lichfield Close because the home of Dr Erasmus Darwin was adjacent to that approach (a member of the Lunar Society and grandfather to Charles Darwin).

Dud's Civil War

As a royalist under Charles I, valiant Dud entered Civil War strife and told how he was "in most of the Battailes that year." Present at Edgehill and the siege of Worcester, he was characterised as both quaint and loyal, telling many

282 Dudley Metropolitan, 'Woodsetton Township'.

283 Staffordshire, *Collections for a History of Staffordshire*, 'The Civil War in Staffordshire in the Spring of 1646: Sir William Brereton's Letter Book, April-May 1646'.

stories of his war adventures, of serving with the troops of Prince Maurice and escaping imprisonment.[284]

Earlier, Dud rose to General Ordnance under Maurice whose brother, Rupert of the Rhine, was of a scientific bent and was a Member of the Royal Society. He tried to smelt iron from coal in Sussex unsuccessfully. It's probable that he came into contact with Dud's ideas. Dud's life story was described as romantic. Really? Any volunteers for re-living his troubled days? War is not good news for anyone but Dud was still suffering from dreadful luck and matters continued badly for him:

> "Ironworks destroyed;
> Property confiscated;
> Sickly wife without shelter;
> Dud himself in Worcester prison facing death."

Princes Maurice and Rupert suffered too as both brothers were banished after the fall of Oxford in June 1646. Dud escaped to Bristol in 1648 with help from Major Elliotts, who overpowered the warder.

Charles I – regicide, 30 January 1649

Charles I was beheaded by axe outside Whitehall Palace. Dismayed crowds were held back from the scaffold by troops on horseback.[285] Dud remained unfindable in Bristol until after it had happened.[286] Following the regicide, Dud made another attempt to establish iron works near Bristol but there had been a disagreement with his business partner. By 1665, he described himself as being at Green's Lodge:

> "near which are four forges – Green's Forge, Swin Forge, Heath Forge, and Cradley Forge – where I practice my invention."

William Dugdale 'the Herald' (appointed to Staffordshire) interviewed Edward Parkhouse and his nephew Dud Dudley separately in 1663. Their

---

284 Carl Higgs, *Sedgley Men of Iron: Dud Dudley and Abraham Darby – Keeping it in the Family!*

285 Peter Ackroyd, *The Civil War* (2014), pp.309-310.

286 John Alfred Langford, et al., 'The Rise and Progress of the Manufacturers of Staffordshire'.

genealogies were recorded and coats of arms. John Darby (Derby of Sedgley) was interviewed too. Two years later, Edward (alt. Parkhouse) urged Dud to write his treatise *Metallum Martis*. Dud was responsible also for a geological survey of Dudley and its environs. From Dud's perspective, he named Edward as one of the few people he would trust with his method of smelting iron from pit-coal. Edward contributed to Robert Plot's *Natural History of Staffordshire* and gave sight of significant geological sites within his ownership at Lower Gornal.[287]

Had the charcoal iron forgers listened to Dud back in 1618 and not barred pit-coal, much wood would have been preserved.[288] Copies of Dud Dudley's *Metallum Martis* went to The British Museum. Himley Hall had an original edition.[289] Numerous subscribers were listed, including:

	copies
"E. Elwell, Esq., of Wednesbury Forge –	2
Lord Ward, Witley Court, Worcestershire –	6
H. Ward, Esq., Wolverhampton –	3
John Richards Esq., Wolverhampton –	1
Birmingham Library –	1

> This long list was signed by Late W. Baldwin Esq. of the Ellowes Sedgley [who] had a manuscript copy of Dud Dudley's book 'which he kindly lent to the editor'.
>
> 'The Publisher to the Reader' signed by John N. Bagnall."

Dud Dudley was aware of a John Richards and the Elwells too and they were aware of him; the Richards and Elwells are of this saga: direct descendants of Dud's parents were to marry into these families. Dud annexed a short pedigree to "shew the family of Dud Dudley." He dedicated very politely to the "Kings Most Sacred Majesty" but made sure to write:

---

287 Carl Higgs, *Sedgley Men of Iron: Dud Dudley and Abraham Darby – Keeping it in the Family!*

288 John Alfred Langford, et al., 'The Rise and Progress of the Manufacturers of Staffordshire'.

289 Dud Dudley, *Metallum Martis* (1665, reprint 1851).

> "And a Loyal suffere, for Your Sacred Majesty..."

In *The Epistle* pages 9, 11 and 33 he speaks three times of Pit-coal, Sea-coal, Peat and Turff. The names Turvey and Turley apply to turf workers, this might be the case with this saga's Turleys. He mentions his father on pages 4-5 and there is a letter on p.5, which begins:

> "Son Dudley,
>
> The Kings Majesty being at New Market, I sent Parkes thither on Saturday to some Friends of mine, to move the Kings Majesty for my Pattent..."

Fleeing Regicides

The King had increasingly become the 'bete-noir' of North American preachers as well; the dispute between Britain and its colonies had worsened.[290] *Regicides on the Run* is described by reviewer Vallance as "certainly the stuff of excellent history." The book is about the signatories of Charles I's death warrant, Edward Whalley and William Goffe, who fled to New England, America, after the restoration of the monarchy in 1660. Their fellow 'regicide' was John Dixwell. For New England Puritan ministers, such as Jonathan Mayhew, the 'regicides' "were not king-killers but men who had shown legitimate resistance towards a tyrant."

Commonwealth, 1649-1660

Oliver Cromwell acted as head of state and head of government of the new republican commonwealth, influenced by the Earls of Warwick and Holland.

Battle of Worcester, 3 September 1651

This was the final battle of the English Civil War. Cromwell's New Modern Army pressed 28,000 men against around 14,000 mainly Scots supporters, who marched south to defend would-be Charles II, led by David Leslie of Dunbar. After the Battle, Charles fled, via Stourbridge and Wordsley, bound

---

290 Matthew Jenkinson, *Regicides on the Run, Charles I's Killers in America: the Lives & Afterlives of Edward Whalley & William Goffe* (Oxford, 2019). Reviewed by Edward Vallance (2020). *https://literaryreview.co.uk/regicides-on-the-run* [accessed 9 August 2020].

for Boscobel. In busy Stourbridge, his party dismounted their horses and mingled amongst French-speaking Huguenot glassmakers. The royal group were able to speak to each other in French as they crossed the town, easily blending with the population. Charles sought refuge at Boscobel and Moseley Old Hall (between Cannock and Wednesfield, Wolverhampton).

At last the raging Civil War ended, an estimated 127,000 people had died with consequent plagues and famines. On a social level, the battles advanced artisan and working classes to the detriment of higher-born powers. Westminster Government turned fairer as royal sovereignty became answerable to Parliament. The impact on the whole general population around the British Isles was extreme.[291]

Old Park and Wren's Nest

In 1649 a detailed survey of Dudley landowners had been undertaken. It revealed that Groves Land was on the Rowley Regis side where Richard Parkes (or Parkhouse) owned meadows by the side of the mill stream at Windmill End. Higgs like Taplin finds that there was a gamekeeper's lodge standing in the "Old Park" of Dudley and Sedgley, part of the private game reserve owned by Dudley lords.[292] John Bagley, Elizabeth Tomlinson's nephew, was recorded as "head deer-keeper" as early as 1611. He was granted "the ancient lodge" in "Old Park" as his home the same year. With a Dudley boundary south side and the Sedgley-Dudley Road west side, Woodsetton Township, Sedgley, comprised three settlements: Flaxhalls, Turls Hill and Parks Hall. The association with Woodsetton Old Park and Wrens Nest went back to the 16th century. The Sedgley Parish Register makes reference to keepers of Old Park being named Fellows.

Humble Ward and his wife Frances lived at Wren's Nest House in the Old Park, which was assumed to have come to them from her father Ferdinando Sutton Dudley. Sure enough, Humble leased the Old Park Estate, minus Wren's Nest House, for 21 years to John Darby in December 1649. Another document showed that John was living there still in 1683. It was the only habitable place on the estate. John's daughter with wife Margaret was born and baptised in Sedgley Church 1651. They had another girl later, Esther.

291 History Collection, 5, *Bolton Massacre, 1644*, illus. *https://historycollection.com* [accessed 24 July 2020].

292 Carl Higgs, *Sedgley Men of Iron: Dud Dudley and Abraham Darby – Keeping it in the Family!*

Richard, their son, came in 1655 and eventually married and delivered Abraham Darby I.[293] [294] Thus the Abraham Darbys were many generations removed saga first cousins from Jane Persehouse (b. Sutton Dudley's line) an amazing branch of the tree; the Darbys were not direct saga ancestors.

From Taplin's work, it is known that Colonel Charles M. Hansen contributed an article to *The American Genealogist* entitled 'The Ancestry of William and Ann (Bagley) Brinton', in which he discussed the origins of the Brinton and Bagley families of Dudley. The Colonel built on previous research, especially concerning a William Brinton and Ann Bagley, who married circa 1659. They were thought to be early Quakers, which could explain why the parish records carry no record of their marriage. A Friends' ceremony of 1659 is believed to have taken place.[295] [296]

Charles II – reigned King of Scotland from 1649-1651 (last coronation at Scone), King of Scotland, England and Ireland from the 1660 Restoration – 1685

In 1660 the Long Parliament voted for its own dissolution. Charles II established a honeymoon period with the provincial lauded classes. Dud reminded the King that his house in Worcester had been given up for the service of Charles I and had been turned into a factory for arms. This was Dud's 2nd petition and appeared to be unsuccessful, like the petitions of so many other disgruntled people. Staffordshire local authorities compiled lists of ex-parliamentarian soldiers and their places of abode and forwarded details to Whitehall. Such documents show that deputy lieutenants were connected with central authority and colleagues in counties.

The Civil War cost Richard Leveson (1598-1661), godson to his Elizabethan namesake, all his wealth – his personal estate was worth £24,000. Also, he lost four fifths of the proceeds from his coal and mine works to Parliamentary coffers. He had been neutral in the 1st Civil War and royalist later. There was a further demand on him set at £9,846: "greater than many

293 Dudley Metropolitan, 'Woodsetton Township'.

294 Hannah Rose, 'Abraham Darby of Coalbrookdale', (memoirs, records that Abraham Darby lived at Wren's Nest).

295 Janetta W. Schoonover, *Brinton Genealogy. A History of William Brinton who came from England to Chester County* (America) (1924).

296 John Taplin, *Shakespeare's Granddaughter and the Bagleys of Dudley*. Charles M. Hansen, 'The Ancestry of William and Ann Brinton', *The American Genealogist*. *http://www.brintonfamily.org*

earls and noblemen" he protested. By surrendering six rectories he eventually reduced that figure to £3,846 and ordered what remained of his estate to be conveyed to trustees acting for his wife for 21 years after his death. Thereafter, his lands were to descend to his niece, Margaret and her husband Francis Fowler. Fowler is another surname descending timewise into this Staffordshire family but Margaret's maiden name is unknown.

The Fitton's old home, Gawsworth Hall, was remodelled in 1701 and was acquired by the Richards family in 1962. There are Richards in this saga too, who may or may not be related to the same family.[297]

On the Restoration of the Monarchy, Edward Hyde had returned to England and Charles II gave him the title Earl of Clarendon and appointed him Lord Chancellor. As a Member of Parliament, he had strongly criticised Charles I and had supported the impeachment of Thomas Wentworth, Earl of Stafford, however Hyde had changed sides in 1641 to support the royalists and stayed with the King in Oxford. He had been appointed as an adviser to Charles II in exile in 1646.[298] Later in this saga, there are Hydes of various statuses.

Much commented on by Pepys and others, no book was so much read as Butler's *Hudibras*. After Newport Pagnell was garrisoned in 1645, it was rumoured to be the *Hudibras* of Butler. Everyone in the court of Charles II felt duty bound to be familiar with this burlesque poem. From the palace it swept into chocolate-houses and taverns alike. Lord Chancellor Hyde promised Butler rewards and hung his portrait within his library.[299]

Alfred Young argued that persons of the New England press attacked British rule in the colonies using pseudonyms of Whalley and Goffes – '*noms de plume*'. The real pair eluded the Crown agent's reach because Charles II realised that pursuing remaining 'regicides' could backfire. Thirteen were executed between 1660 and 1662 and were emerging as martyrs of the 'Good Old Cause'. The King did not want any rallying, he knew such deaths could stir political and religious dissidence. Furthermore, Massachusetts Bay Colony and New Haven

297 *History of Parliament: The House of Commons 1604-1629*, 'Leveson, Richard (1598-1661), of Whorne's Place, Cuxton, Kent; Lilleshall Lodge, Salop and Trentham, Staffs; later of Boswell Court, nr. St. Clement's Well, London', ed. Andrew Thrush and John P. Ferris (Cambridge, 2010). Fn. 24 Staffs. RO, D593/C/13. Fn. 43 PROB 11/315, ff. 12-15v.

298 John Simkin, *Edward Hyde, Earl of Clarendon*.

299 Samuel Butler, Metre of *Hudibras* (a burlesque poem which became popular all over the land).

were respectively governed in the early 1660s by John Endecott and William Leete. They were unsympathetic with the monarchy and lacked motivation when it came to capturing 'regicides'. The name Leete again![300]

Catherine, born Princess of Denmark, was said to have been ostracised by Danish royals possibly for her first marriage to Simeone Leete or due to her second marriage, following widowhood, to John Turley of Sedgley. This American aspect is quite a find because this John (1575-1661) and his son with Catherine, John (1604-1661), both died on the same day: 2 February 1661. It seemed like family researchers were mistaking the two records but no-one knew the causes of death, an event in common seemed most likely. From 6 January 1661, a Nonconformist dissenting group of 50 members called the Fifth Monarchists, headed by wine-cooper Thomas Venner, were either killed or taken prisoner. On 19 January, Venner and ten others were hung, drawn and quartered for high treason.[301] Is this just a coincidence? The coronation of Charles II took place on 23 April 1661. Discovering William Leete of Massachusetts in a powerful position during the early 1660s points very much to sudden violence against the two Johns. Also, it brings into doubt the likelihood of Catherine having been in Queen Anne's company. Rather, it suggests that Catherine did not revive relations with her family of birth after they removed or distanced her.

In 1660, Elias Ashmole gave Dud a reference for practising as an able doctor in Worcester. Dud retired to St. Helen's seemingly to find a quieter life. Surprisingly, he was granted a licence on 30 July 1679 to practice medicine in the 'province' of Canterbury.[302] His inventive endeavours had spanned most of his previous years. The due reward of his "lofty enterprise and unquenchable zeal" may have eluded him in his lifetime, however, it subsequently formed the foundation of Staffordshire iron trading.[303]

Dud died aged 85 in 1684, he was buried at St. Helen's, the same church as his wife.

---

300 Matthew Jenkinson, *Regicides on the Run, Charles I's Killers in America.*

301 Thomas Venner, 'Daily entries from the 17th century London diary', *The Diary of Samuel Pepys. https://www.pepysdiary.com/encyclopaedia/1777* [accessed 22 February 2021]. *The Diary of Samuel Pepys* (Saturday 19 January, 1661).

302 Carl Higgs, *Sedgley Men of Iron: Dud Dudley and Abraham Darby – Keeping it in the Family!* Addendum: Martin White, 'Yet another side of Dud Dudley' in *Blackcountryman* (magazine), vol. 39, issue 3, (Summer, 2006).

303 John Alfred Langford, et al., 'The Rise and Progress of the Manufacturers of Staffordshire'.

From a first column in St. Helen's Church, Worcester:

> "Dodo Dudley chiarchi mobilis Edwardi nuper domini de Dudley filias… saepe captus anno 1648."

From another column:

> "On the top a lion rampant, later destroyed."[304]

Dud deserved accolades. Even Dud's earlier monument had been destroyed by 1863.[305]

Onward religions

Dudley's local Catholic recusants had been excommunicated in 1674, including Henry Juckes, whose name had been on a list of 43 dissenters in 1676 too. Shakespeare was not an uncommon surname in Dudley, Roger Shakespeare being amongst members of the congregation of St. Thomas's who were on the 1676 list prepared by Churchwardens. By 1679, the list of 'popish recusants' included Henry, his wife Mary, and their son James Juckes. Chitham describes Edward Elwell as one of St. Thomas's churchwardens that year.[306] Many of the dissenters were thought to be 'popish recusants' attending a church in Sedgley. John Bayliss was absent from St. Edmund's, Dudley but might have been influenced to pray elsewhere by so-called 'foreign' Christian Lewis.

There was a marriage settlement between Philip Tomlinson and Frances Bayles, dated 1684. It's possible that Philip Tomlinson was a descendant of the 1560s born John or James Tomlinson, both were likely to have benefited from Elizabeth and Ann Tomlinson's proximity to nobility and seem to have been upwardly mobile.[307] As previously stated, the eldest daughter of Edward Bagley (senior), Ann Bagley, moved to Pennsylvania around 1684 with her

304 Treadwell Russell Nash, *Collections for the history of Worcestershire, vol 2*, (London, 1799), 2 vols.

305 S. Smiles, *Industrial Biography.*

306 Edward Chitham, *The Story of Dudley*, p.74.

307 Barnard Family of South Cave, Hull (The papers of the Barnard family arrived as two deposits): John or James Tomlinson information (1560s). Section U DDBA2 (1541-1886) Marriage settlement of Philip Tomlinson and Frances Bayles (1684). (There was a section of wills also in DDBAZ (1812-1890) containing John Dennis (1878) regarding his tenancy).

Quaker husband William Brinton and their children, except for their Ann, who initially remained in England with her husband John Bennett.[308]

James II of England, VII of Scotland – reigned 1685-1689

James II acceded to the crown of his unexpectedly deceased brother Charles II in 1685, leaving 13 illegitimate heirs, including Henry Fitzroy, 1st Duke of Grafton (1663-1690) by Barbara Villiers, Duchess of Cleveland. Only aged 27, Fitzroy was killed in the storming of Cork, Ireland, during a Jacobite War of 1690.

Henry VIII had an illegitimate child, with beauty Lady Elizabeth (Bessie) Blount of Kinlet (minor Shropshire gentry descended from the Mountjoys). Their son Henry Fitzroy (1519-1536) lived to be only 17 years old.

In 1660, James II married eight months pregnant Anne Hyde, who died 11 years later. They had two daughters: Mary, who married William of Orange and Anne, who married George, son of the King of Denmark. Both were Protestants, both decided their half-brother, born to their step-mother Mary of Modena in 1688, James Francis Edward, was a foundling imposter, capable of securing a Catholic succession for the Stuarts.

The Glorious Revolution, 1688-1689

William of Orange landed 15,000 in England to save Protestantism. Deposed, James II raced to France.

William III (of Orange) – reigned 1689-1702 with Mary II 1689-1694

William defeated James II finally at the Battle of the Boyne in Ireland. James returned to France. England now had a constitutional monarchy answerable to Parliament. William and Mary (b. Hyde) ruled jointly as King and Queen of England, Scotland and Ireland. Mary died of smallpox in 1694 and James II died in St. Germain-en-Laye near Paris in 1701. Mary's sister Anne would be Queen.[309]

---

308 John Taplin, *Shakespeare's Granddaughter and the Bagleys of Dudley*, 'Biographical sketches: the testimony of William Brinton concerning the life and death of his dear wife', *Friend Magazine*.

309 *Kings and Queens of the British Isles*, ed. Thomas Cussans, *The Times* (London, 2015), illus., maps, pp.148-153.

Queen Anne – reigned 1702-1714

The formal union of England and Scotland commenced in 1707 at which point Queen Anne became the first monarch of Great Britain. Her short reign saw victories in the Spanish War of Succession under General John Churchill, created Duke of Marlborough in 1702. Sadly, Anne had 13 stillborn children and without an heir she was the last Stuart Protestant monarch. Despite there being numerous Stuarts with better claims to the throne, Parliament chose to support Hanoverians. Sophia of Hanover was Protestant and granddaughter of James I but she had died two years before Anne. Her eldest son George Augustus had intentionally become an English subject from 1705 so that, whatever happened, the British throne would pass smoothly to him, assured by the *Act of Settlement* of 1701.[310]

As far as this saga goes, it was commercial expansion that was increasingly important to livelihoods. John Darby senior benefited from his son's success at Coalbrookdale. He relocated to Madeley Lodge with his daughter Esther and husband Anthony Parker around 1706 and lived a long life. Margaret's grandson Abraham Darby born at Wren's Nest, Dudley (1678-1717) was the first person to produce iron commercially using coke instead of charcoal at his works in Coalbrookdale, Shropshire, in 1709.[311]

310 Parliament, *Act of Settlement* (1701).

311 Dud Dudley and Abraham Darby, 'Forging new Links'. Retrieved by Black Country Society, (28 May 2015).

Chapter 6

Forward Families?

MOVING INTO the British Hanoverian era, which began in 1714, this saga's Sutton Dudley, Tomlinson and Persehouse lines gave way to five main surnames (and their alternatives) presented here in alphabetical order:

Darby
Elwell
Richards
Turley
Wilkes

The Darbys

The Darbys were generations removed saga first cousins from Jane Persehouse (b. Sutton Dudley's line) an interesting branch of the tree at this stage of the saga although the Darbys were not direct ancestors.

With a Dudley boundary south side and the Sedgley-Dudley Road west side, Woodsetton Township, Sedgley, comprised three settlements: Flaxhalls, Turls Hill, and Parks Hall.[312] The association with Woodsetton Old Park and Wrens Nest went back to the 16th century. The Sedgley Parish Register makes reference to keepers of Old Park being named Fellows. Humble Ward

312 Dudley Metropolitan Borough Council, 'Township of Sedgley 1750', produced by John Hemingway and Jennifer Foster (Dudley, 2006), bibliog. col. map, pdfs. *https://www.dudley.gov.uk/residents/planning/historic-environment/historic-maps-of-dudley/* [accessed 16 October 2020]. (Dudley's historic maps can be viewed from 1307 to the present day). 'Woodsetton Township'.

and his wife Frances lived at Wren's Nest House in the Old Park, which was assumed to have come to them from her father Ferdinando Dudley Sutton (alt. Sutton Dudley). Humble leased the Old Park Estate, minus Wren's Nest House, for 21 years to John Darby in December 1649. Another document showed that John was living there still in 1683. It was the only habitable place on the estate. John's daughter with wife Margaret was born and baptised in Sedgley Church 1651, they had another girl later, Esther. Richard, their son, arrived in 1655 and eventually married and delivered Abraham Darby I.[313]

About 1745, ironmasters of Staffordshire began to benefit from Dud Dudley's enterprise. By a series of renewed experiments undertaken by Abraham Darby II of Coalbrookdale (1711-1763) and John Wilkinson of Bradley, the smelting of iron with coal became an established improvement for which Wilkinson deserved the major credit in Langford's opinion.[314] The Abraham Darby I to III comprised:

Abraham I	Produced coke-smelted pig suitable for cast iron but not wrought iron;
Abraham II	Smelted pig iron with coke to produce wrought iron;
Abraham III	Built the world's first iron bridge across the Severn.[315]

English landed society still held on to respected traditional status and prestige. For this reason, newly wealthy merchants, manufacturers, traders and those in emerging occupations found themselves socially adrift. The Abraham Darbys and others with new money tended to adopt Quaker and Unitarian dissenting religious beliefs. It meant that often third generations were the first to be acceptable to English society. This was achieved by conforming and adapting enough to the central value system, including a return to Anglicism for some.[316]

---

313 Hannah Rose, 'Abraham Darby of Coalbrookdale', (memoirs, records that Abraham Darby lived at Wren's Nest).

314 John Alfred Langford, et al., 'The Rise and Progress of the Manufacturers of Staffordshire' in *Staffordshire and Warwickshire Past and Present* (London and Birmingham, printed 1884), vol. 1., p.xxii, illus. from original drawings by H. Warren.

315 John Watney, *The Industrial Revolution*, Pitkin, (n.d.), b.&w. and col. illus.

316 Arnold Thackray, 'Natural knowledge in cultural content: The Manchester Mode' in *The American Historical Review*, vol. 79, issue 3, (June, 1974), pp.679-680 of 672-709.

Abraham Darby III (1750-1789) commenced working in Coalbrookdale in 1768. There were three ironworks that belonged to the family then: Coalbrookdale and Horsehay both had two blast furnaces; Ketley had three. There were forges at Coalbrookdale and Bridgnorth. The Coalbrookdale's partners' mining lands swept from Donnington in North Shropshire south to the Severn, plus they owned farms in Madeley. During Darby III's time, the company expanded yet more. His personal account books survived, which left more information than was known about his father and grandfather. In 1777 he bought a wig while his stockings were obtained on visits to London. Newspapers and magazines were regularly purchased compared with irregularly bought chocolate and cocoa from Quaker Joseph Fry in Bristol. Coalbrookdale was the most applauded industrial region in the country. Most innovations of the Industrial Revolution that needed iron were connected with the area.[317]

William Reynolds (1758-1803) was Abraham Darby II's grandson, making Abraham III his uncle. William was the brains behind the Shropshire tub-boat canal system. He surveyed the route and managed its construction. Eventually, the controlling shareholders of the Coalbrookdale Company were the surviving females of Abraham Darby II's family; Deborah, widow of son Samuel, and Rebecca, widow of Abraham III. The Iron Bridge was a curiosity at first but after its first decade, in the early 1790s, others were designing similar constructions, notably architect John Nash and philosopher Tom Paine. Trinder wrote of the flood affecting the Severn in a 1795 winter storm when one newspaper had reported how the Iron Bridge had: "Firmly stood and dauntless braved the storm."

Cast iron window frames were produced at Coalbrookdale too: St. Alkmund's Church, Shrewsbury, received such window frames in the Gothic style around 1793-1795. Apart from architectural iron products, bridges and steam engines, Coalbrookdale dealt in highly varied goods, from making power mill beds for creating gunpowder to domestic bookcases and clock weights.[318]

Ann Darby, born in Madeley (1779-1840), was daughter of Abraham III and Rebecca; she married Barnard Dickinson in 1805. His parents

---

317 Barrie Trinder, *The Darbys of Coalbrookdale*, 1974 rev. ed. (Chichester, 1991), pp.26-45, illus., map, Figure 1, The Darby Family Tree (Simplified).

318 B. Trinder, *The Darbys of Coalbrookdale*, 1974 rev. ed. (Chichester, 1991).

were John Dickinson and Mary (born Barnard). A cousin, Edmund Darby, died in 1810. The Barnards of Coalbrookdale relate back to Ann and John Bagley's descendants, beginning with Edward Bagley (called "lovable kin" by Shakespeare's granddaughter Lady Elizabeth Barnard). There were other associated Barnard lines of Atherton and Nether Winchendon plus East Riding. The Cave family of Baggrave, Leicestershire seemed to be linked too. In 1480, East Riding Officer, Walter Taverner was related to Tomlinson. Mayors of Durham included the names Barnard and Fowler between 1741-1968, saga names. This saga contains at least one Barnard Tomlinson.

Edmund Darby (1782-1810) and his wife Lucy were parents to Abraham Darby IV (1804-1878). Edmund's friends were James Watt and the Fletchers, their common interest being steam cylinders.[319] When Edmund died, Barnard Dickinson, who married Ann Darby, became manager of Coalbrookdale Ironworks. In the early 1780s, a forge was built at Horsehay, which was at first powered by water but later by steam power. At Ketley a new entirely steam-powered forge began production in 1785. The Coalbrookdale partners networked with Matthew Boulton as well as James Watt, whose improved steam engines began service in 1776. In 1781-1782 Newcomen's pumping engine at Coalbrookdale was replaced by Boulton & Watt's steam engine *Resolution*.[320]

Elwell family (alts. Ellow, Ellown, Elwall)

The Elwells were a prominent family in the Black Country and were amongst the founding fathers of the Industrial Revolution. Two books were written by J.L. Elwell, the second is a collection of letters edited by him. He had an outstanding career as a counter-espionage officer for UK MI5, responsible in 1961 for breaking the Portland spy ring, run by the KGB officer Konon Molody (Gordon Lonsdale), which passed naval secrets to the Russians. A year later Elwell had similar success with John Vassall, the KGB spy at the Admiralty. He died aged 88 in January 2008.[321] [322]

319 Charles E.G. Pease, *The Descendants of John Darby* (19 November 2015). Pennyghael, Isle of Mull, Pennyghael.org.uk/Darby.pdf [accessed 6 August 2016], 78 citations.

320 B. Trinder, *The Darbys of Coalbrookdale*, 1974 rev. ed. (Chichester, 1991).

321 Charles J.L. Elwell, *The Iron Elwells; A Family Social History*, 2nd ed., rev. and enlarged, (Ilfracombe, Devon, 1992), illus.

322 *A Lady of Wednesbury Forge: The Diary of Georgina Elwell* (covering 1868-1869), edited by C.J.L. Elwell, new and revised ed., (Black Country, 2011), Illus.

Aelle (alt. Aella) reputedly headed the Elwell charts in *Iron Elwells* as he gave his name to the Vale of Sedgley and was fabled to have been a descendant of Woden. According to the *Anglo Saxon Chronicle,* Woden's direct descendant was Sigegar. Sigegar's glade could have become Sigegarsley and then Seggesley and then Sedgley.[323] *The Dictionary of National Biography* described Aella as King from AD 559-588 of the ancient kingdom of Deira, Eastern Yorkshire. When Aelle died, his second son ruled Deira. Aelle came to the ear of Pope Gregory the Great when he asked, at the Rome slave market, which tribe of Angles a certain group of slaves were from. He was told that they were from Deira ruled by Aelle. His response was that *Allelujah* should be sung to that land. Much has been learnt from archaeology since 1992 when *Iron Elwells* was published.

Map of Northumbria around 700 AD showing the ancient kingdom of Deira.

King Aelle was amongst the legendary founders of royal Anglo-Saxon dynasties who were merely leaders in times of war not peace. Adams writes that to call them Kings is to flatter them. Bede allows such men no more than the term *duces*. The idea of a people choosing or appointing a *dux* just for the duration of a military campaign follows the ancestral Germanic tradition of a war leader who stood down afterwards. This concept had been replaced by the 7th century when a King permanently remained.

As a Deiran wife, Aelle's daughter Acha could bear sons fit to rule all of the English north of the Humber, according to the *British Historical Miscellany* compiled by a 9th century historian known as Nennius.[324] Aethelfrith joined the two ancient lands of Bernicia and Deira together into one kingdom north of the Humber. He and his father appear in the Anglo-Saxon Chronicle under entry 588 as the successor of Aelle. In 866 a civil war raged between an Aella and his brother Osberht in Northumbria. The Danes took advantage of the situation, crossed the Humber estuary, to capture York on 1 November.

323 Charles J.L. Elwell, *The Iron Elwells. Anglo Saxon Chronicle.*

324 *British Historical Miscellany,* compiled by Nennius.

The two brothers retaliated, both were killed on 21 March, 867.[325] Further relevant history earlier than 1066 can be found.[326] [327] [328] [329] [330] [331] [332]

The Burges of Dudley Assize Roll 1274-1275 records that an Elias Ewayn acquired *liber de Burgo* – freedom of the town. Could this have been Ellown or Elwell?[333] It is likely that part of Sedgley was held by the Ellowes or Elwalls from at least the first written record of 1327 (concerning Adam de Ellewalle's subsidy dues). A man named Adam de Ellewalle was a Sedgley juror in 1378. Charles Elwell speculated that Adam could have been descended from a son of King Aella (reigned 559-588).[334]

From *Domesday*, we know that William FitzAnsculf's vassal Ralph of Ellesborough was Lord of nearby Wombourne Manor.[335] Adam's ancestors probably took their name from Sedgley's Ellenvale garden and moor (Aelle's vale), the exact positions although uncertain were claimed to be located in Sedgley near Dudley in the vicinity of Ellowes Road and Ellowes Row. On the ground where Ellowes Hall would be built in the 1800s, there lies a 'sugar well', so called because of the sweet taste of its water, likely to be rich in minerals. The name Elwell is not attributed to a well origin however, it is believed to have come from arrow-making or archery practice (against a wall). From *Iron Elwells* we find that the good ell length of a dart, arrow or clothyard shaft had been a play on words or 'in joke' within Elwell family tradition.

An aside while on the subject of estates. By the 18th century the aristocracy expressed their wealth and status by proudly showing off wide areas of parkland

---

325 Sarah Zaluckyj and John Zaluckyj 'Decline' in Sarah Zaluckyj, *Mercia: The Anglo-Saxon Kingdom of Central England* (2001), ch. 10, p.243.

326 Max Adams, *In the Land of Giants: Journeys Through the Dark Ages* (London, 2015).

327 Max Adams, *The King in the North* (London, 2013).

328 Chronicle of John of Worcester, compilation (1124-1140). 'Vita Walderi' (legend). Earl of Ulf, Denmark, m. King Canute's sister Estrith (Siward's first cousin).

329 H.S. Grazebrook, *The Barons of Dudley*, vol. IX (Stafford, 1888).

330 *Open Domesday*, the first free online copy of the Domesday Book. Data created by J.J.N. Palmer, University of Hull. Site by Anne Powell-Smith. *http://opendomesday.org* [accessed 17 March 2017].

331 *The 'Anglian Collection' of royal genealogies*, compiled by Keith Fitzpatrick-Matthews (2000-2006 last updated 27.2.2006), [Accessed 4 October 17].

332 *Sutton-Breasley family*, Brown Co., Ohio.

333 Dudley Public Libraries, edited by J.S. Roper. (Transcript series).

334 Charles J.L. Elwell, *The Iron Elwells*, pp.18-19.

335 *Open Domesday*, Ellesborough lordship (Phillimore) Ref. 17.2 Manor 2 [also [17.3 Manor 3].

that surrounded their stately homes. Himley Village was ambitiously relocated completely, including the church being re-erected on its present site in 1764. Over ten years later, John Ward (d.1788) brought in Lancelot 'Capability' Brown to re-design the parkland. Archaeological evidence points to Lancelot's son-in-law, architect Henry Holland, as being responsible for improvements to the Hall around the same time. Between 1823-1833 William Atkinson, a famous London architect, covered the external walls with his special cement rendering on behalf of 4th Viscount Dudley and Ward.[336]

A direct Elwell line is found in this saga back to William Elwall (1490-1540), son of John and Jane and married to another Jane (born circa 1500), 15th generation direct ancestor to the author. William and Jane Elwell (b. Jennings) were also 14th generation ancestors, both parents born circa 1620. Their son was Richard "of the Swyrd of Sedgley" (alt. surname Ellow, 1541-1621) and his wife Rose (1545-1622), 13th generation direct ancestors.

A Stephen Elwell born 1588 was 78 in 1666, with 12 children, which included two pairs of twins of which one in four survived. *Iron Elwells* tells us that Thomas Parkes (alt. Persehouse) was described as one of the richest men in Staffordshire, who paid 17s 6d in tax in 1655 whereas one of the leading inhabitants of Sedgley, Oliver Elwell, paid only 2s 4d. Oliver and his wife had twins to raise plus six other children. Oliver (1593-1663) of Tot More, Ettingshall, was a leading inhabitant of Sedgley, his will was proved at Sedgley Manor Court. Sedgley has been home to the Elwells for centuries. There are numerous examples of alternative spellings of the surname. Sedgley people were very fond of assigning nicknames too, just as our folk did.

John Elwall at Hurst Hill (1626-1692), on a list of active Parliamentarians in the Civil War, was on the Parish Council and was also a churchwarden at Sedgley (1677). He paid only one hearth tax in 1666 and died in 1692, there were eight children. His son referred to lands his father had recently purchased from Thomas Wilks, co-heirs in Ettingshall. Churchwardens were regarded as gentlemen. In 1676 Roger Shakespeare was amongst members of the congregation of St. Thomas's who were on a list of dissenters prepared by churchwardens. By 1679 the list had grown to 43 people, including John Baylies and a Susanna. Many of the dissenters were thought to be 'popish recusants' attending a church in Sedgley. Edward Elwell was a churchwarden

336 Dudley Council, *History of Himley Hall*, handout.

of St. Thomas's, which makes it probable that the Elwells knew the Bayliss family well and were possibly at religious odds with them around that time. John Bayliss was absent from St. Edmund's too but might have been influenced to pray elsewhere by so-called 'foreign' Christian Lewis.[337] Parsons explained that St. Edmund's was destroyed by defending royalists in the English Civil War and was rebuilt in 1724.[338] Meanwhile, the spire of St. Thomas 'Top Church' pointed high into the sky; the two churches combined before 1724.

Intertwined Elwell, Richards, Tomlinsons, Turleys, Wilkes surnames

On 14 May 1656 a Mr Wilkes lived at Wapping Dock when Dudley's boundaries were being checked after the Civil War. Unfortunately, in 1779 a Selmon Wilkes caused people problems underfoot by leaving a hole leading to his cellar open along a Dudley footpath. Chitham wrote that in October 1793, Edward Parkes was one of 11 householders (another was Benjamin Jackson) who were asked to remove nuisances such as penthouses and obstructive windows from their houses in High Street, Dudley and it seems that these requests were carried out.[339]

The Turleys, Wilkes, Tomlinsons and Elwells were intertwined over generations. During the 1700s two generations of Richards (surname) came into the lines. Mary Persehouse (1696-1727) married Thomas Richards (circa 1694-1734). He was descended from the Mintridge family of Nether Gornal, Sedgley; his father-in-law emigrated to Missouri, America. Thomas Richards was married more than once, his child with Mary was direct ancestor Sarah Louisa Richards (1719-1780) of Sedgley, who married Richard Turley (1715-1794). That couple's grandchild was Daniel Elwell (bapt. 1754). The Turleys were descendants of the Wilkes family, found in this saga back to William Wilkes, born 1549, with a son of the same name known to have married Elizabeth Ellown (alt. Ellow or Elwall). Likewise, direct ancestor, Edward Wilkes' dates were 1610-1675 along the Elwell tree. Six generations later, Esther (born Turley, bapt. Christmas Day 1756, daughter of Elizabeth Turley b. Parkes) married the previously mentioned Daniel Elwell (b.1754);

---

337 Edward Chitham, *The Story of Dudley* (Stroud, 2014), illus., p.123.

338 Harold Parsons, *Portrait of the Black Country* (London, 1986), p.49.

339 Edward Chitham, *The Story of Dudley* (Stroud, 2014), p.115.

direct ancestors. The wedding took place on 10 October 1776 and their son's name was also Daniel Elwell (b.1781) a nailer. They were another Sedgley family probably of the Woodsetton area. Common but not the commonest Christian names in the area included Daniel and Esther; there were few other Old Testament names in circulation.[340]

Dudley Council published a map entitled *Township of Sedgley,* the geography from 1750 included the following features of the landscape:

Buildings	Mostly in the village and 'The Kilns' by 'Quarry';
Streams	'Pen Brook' and 'Cockle Brook';
Roads	Clearly marked but not named;
Field Boundaries	Bounding majority of land;
Meadow	'Meadow' and 'Bradley's Meadow';
Pasture	'Old High Park', 'Glebe' and 'Foreday's Croft' are examples;
Arable	Majority of land, 'Dicks Piece' and 'Thistly Piece' are examples;
Garden	'Townsend Hall' for example;
Village	East of 'Glebe';
Coppice	'Alder Coppice';
Trees	'Alder Coppice'.

'Ashen Coppice Piece' was pasture. This map shows that the township was predominantly rural with a small urban centre located to the south, slightly west.[341]

Sedgley nailers

The importance of nail making in the area is acknowledged at Dudley's Black Country Living Museum. By the 1500s iron working, particularly nail making, was already a major industry. Thomas Elwell (1636-1716), yeoman and nailer of Ettingshall, gave consent in 1686 to the erection of a pew in Sedgley Church. Daniel Elwall (1650-1731) was the son of Richard Elwell of Coseley, also part of Sedgley, and a nailer. Still young, Daniel found a patron – Thomas

340 Charles J.L. Elwell, *The Iron Elwells*, pp.20-22, 116, 118.

341 Dudley Metropolitan, 'Township of Sedgley 1750'.

Foley of West Bromwich – grandson of Staffordshire ironmaster Richard Foley. In 1682, Elwell was granted a commission to 'seize' iron wire that had been illegally imported. Later in 1699 he attained a customs appointment at the Port of London. His investigation into wine measures resulted in the standardisation of a true wine gallon. He died unrewarded for the extensive work he did for the commissioners of customs but was buried at St. Paul's, Covent Garden, in 1731. Daniel (b.1650) was talented and enterprising; he seems to have spoken well and to have had legal knowledge.[342] Another Daniel Elwell (b.1661) paid 9/7 in rent in 1696/97. That could be 9s 7d or £9 7s, which was regarded as a relatively high sum of rent. At the end of the 17th century, Charles Elwell married Martha, daughter of Thomas Dudley, nailer and gentleman of Tipton and "a member both by birth and marriage of the great house of Dudley." In the 1800s, Dudley was no longer surrounded by fields but by collieries, quarries and ironworks that had begun with nail manufacturing.[343] One early 1800s nail warehouse survived on Brick Street.

The Enlightenment

Jugen Habermas was a continental thinker. His historical analysis linked emerging public institutions with the reconfiguration of private spaces. This insight caused historians of science to relate periodicals and popular texts to the domestic settings in which they were read. Scientific instruments like orreries functioned as household ornaments; consumer culture within bourgeois homes connected with markets for luxury goods.[344] There seems to be no evidence linking the name Orre with orreries, which are mechanical models of the solar system. In the early 1700s, these were notably crafted by George Graham and Thomas Tompion, although orreries were known long back in antiquity. Joseph Wright of Derby (1734-1797) painted *A Philosopher Lecturing on the Orrey* which was exhibited in 1766.

In 1700 Birmingham had no bookseller, yet by the 1790s there were 1,000 in 300 centres. John Baskerville (1706-1775) of Easy Hill, Birmingham, loved typography and experimented with papermaking, typefounding, printing and the manufacture of printers' inks. Baskerville's work resulted in

342 Charles J.L. Elwell, *The Iron Elwells,* pp.22-23.

343 Dudley Metropolitan, 'Dudley Township'.

344 Jan Golinski, 'Science in the Enlightenment, revisited', in *Hist. Sci.*, xlix (2011), pp.217-231, p.220

one typeface bearing his own name in 1754. He triumphed with his *Bible* for Cambridge University Press in 1763, a masterpiece despite the man being a non-believer.[345] While at Cambridge he produced several editions of the *Book of Common Prayer* and *The New Testament* in Greek type that he designed. He improved the way in which metal type was made, which enabled his production of better quality printing, previously impossible.[346] He was "dandy" with "clothes of the most gorgeous description" and he "smothered himself in gold lace…" to be seen "arrayed in a green coat and a scarlet waistcoat."[347] The green was edged with narrow gold lace, the scarlet waistcoat with very broad lace and on his head a hat with a small rim. Queen Anne was on the throne when John Baskerville was born but his lifetime crossed the reigns of King George I, II, III, and IV.

The American scientist and statesman Benjamin Franklin set up a printing business in Philadelphia and visited Birmingham as Baskerville's friend.[348] Also Baskerville was friendly with the Boultons and was indeed a mentor to young Matthew Boulton. Baskerville took part in Birmingham Lunar Society's discussions and was a member of the Royal Society of Arts.[349] [350] Herrmann explored "the enduring legacy of a group of [self-dubbed] 'lunaticks' who kickstarted canal building in Birmingham." Standing in Birmingham Gas Street basin today, almost everything around dates back to the few progressive learned associates who were members of the Lunar Society.[351] Lunar men were so called because they travelled to Birmingham meetings by moonlight from as far as Derby and Lichfield. Some were local: Matthew Boulton, Samuel Galton junior, Joseph Priestley and William Small. James Watt lived in Handsworth and Dr William Withering in Edgbaston. Matthew Boulton helped to get the Birmingham Assay Office opened in 1773, which

---

345 Britain Unlimited, *John Baskerville was an eighteenth-century printer and designer of a typeface which bears his name, www.britainunlimited.com/john-baskerville/* [accessed 16 July 2019]. *Aris's Birmingham Gazette.*

346 Baskerville House, *Birmingham,* Baskerville House handout information sheet.

347 Errol Morris, 'Hear, All Ye People; Hearken, O Earth', *The New York Times.* Fn. 11 Ralph Strauss and Robert Dent, *John Baskerville: A Memoir* (1907), p.11.

348 More about, *John Baskerville* by Bob Miles (2001/2).

349 Francis O'Regan, *John Baskerville (1707-1775) Dandy, Spy, Printer, Atheist? http://brumskeptics.blogspot.com/2011/06/john-baskerville-1706-1775-dandy-spy-.html* [accessed 16 July 2019].

350 *Baskerville House, Birmingham,* Baskerville House handout information sheet.

351 Nicholas Herrmann, 'The Lunar Society' in *Waterfront. A magazine for Friends of the Canal & River Trust,* illus. (Spring/Summer, 2019), issue 9.

meant gold and silver objects no longer had to be hallmarked in Chester and Birmingham's reputation as a city of highly skilled craftsmen grew.[352]

Print was a great engine for the Enlightenment, its boom was a tipping point for learning. The Baconian dictum that knowledge is power remains familiar, whilst less well-known John Dennis, a critic, believed that nothing was more a man's own than his thoughts and inventions. Midlander Samuel Johnson of Lichfield, a poor bookseller's son is much quoted.[353] Here are a few examples, aimed to capture the mood of the time that families would have experienced:

> "General literature now pervades the nation through all its ranks."
>
> "The present age, if we consider chiefly the state of our own country, may be stiled with great propriety, *The Age of Authors.*"
>
> "Grub Street, London, a street near Moorfields much inhabited by writers of small histories, dictionaries, and temporary poems."
>
> "The chief glory of every people arises from its authors."
>
> "Society is held together by communication and information."
>
> "Knowledge is diffused among our people by the news-papers."
>
> "Every house 'supplied with a closet of knowledge'."
>
> "I rejoice to concur with the common reader."
>
> "Before the *Tatler* and *Spectator* England had no mastery of the common life."

Johnson addressing his younger friend and biographer James Boswell (1740-1795):

---

352 Malcolm Dick, *Birmingham; A History of the City and its People* (Birmingham, 2015).

353 Roy Porter, *Enlightenment: Britain and the Creation of the Modern World*, 'Print Culture' (2001), (Allen Lane History), ch. 4, pp.72-95. Fns. 7, 26, 41, 49, 62, 64, 65.

> "Now learning itself is a trade. A man goes to a bookseller, and gets what he can. We have done with patronage."

At last, knowledge was being disseminated to the masses. In 1755, when Johnson's *Dictionary* was published, 2000 copies were printed at a cost of £4 10 shillings.

Edward Elwell known to Johnson and Boswell

Edward Elwell became a Seventh Day Baptist and also caused a stir in London.[354] He was notorious in the 1700s; Dr Samuel Johnson thought he sought notoriety but others doubted that. Edward was brought up in the Church of England. He was born at Ettingshall, Sedgley and moved to Wolverhampton in his twenties where he started as an ironmonger in the town in 1704, but was a grocer, mercer and Constable of the town in 1709. He claimed to know George I and members of the nobility and continued to prosper. By the time of his marriage to Jane Woodward from Birmingham, he was an active Presbyterian. There were numerous Jacobites in Staffordshire (violent against Hanoverian supporters and Nonconformists like Jane and Edward). Jane threw money from the window to 'buy off' a mob, even so Edward came under fire as he rode down Bilston Street (the road connecting Wolverhampton to Sedgley).

Edward Elwell from water colour painted by Carol Biddle based on description in The Iron Elwells.

Edward travelled on business to fairs in different parts of the country. In Bristol, he was converted to Baptism and a minister immersed him and his wife in the Severn. These new Unitarian views prevented him from continuing as a Presbyterian. By then, he was corresponding with the Archbishop

354 Charles J.L. Elwell, *The Iron Elwells,* pp.23-27.

of Canterbury about the doctrine of the Trinity. He pursued heterodoxy as he was at variance with accepted doctrine. His Sabbath was on Saturdays therefore he opened his shop on Sundays; the locals called him "Jew Elwall." He stopped wearing the customary wig and allowed his beard and hair to grow long. He put on a Turkish habit of purple in respect of the Unitarian love for Mohammed. His friend, John Byrom, who wrote the hymn *Christians Awake Salute the Happy Morn*, apparently said that Edward's daughter Lydia would not let him wear a cap or turban made from Josephus that he proposed to put on his head instead of his conventional hat. Byrom asked Lydia whether Edward would wear shoes similar to those of ancient Jews. She replied that the country would be too cold for that. More information was contained in *Byrom's Diary*.

Edward had been a Seventh Day Baptist for ten years, when on 6 December, 1719, he was entered into the Sabbatarian Baptists' Register in London. This was at Mill Yard, Goodmans Fields, Whitechapel. His entry in the register recorded Mr Elwaar of Wolverhampton in Staffordshire. A Mr Hollis and a Mr Dennis were required to report on him. The 'Brothers' enquiries seem to have been acceptable because on 1 May, 1720 "Mr Elwell" was allowed to become "a transient member." He wrote many tracts, the first in 1724; expression of his heretical opinions was extremely offensive to many and he was prosecuted and brought to Stafford Assizes for trial before Judge Denton. Edward wrote his own account, first published in an appendix to a tract in 1736. Sir John Pringle was a physician to George III and a President of the Royal Society. According to his friend Boswell, he had "taken somewhat of a liking to your dissenters and what are now called rational Christians," which was set down in *Boswell for the Defence 1769-1774*.[355] Others present at the trial complimented Elwell's respectful behaviour there and the eloquence of his words in his own defence, which lasted a whole hour. His neighbour Rupert Humpatch, a Wolverhampton JP, testified to his good character. The case was dismissed when Elwell talked of having been in touch with the Archbishop of Canterbury, to which Judge Denton replied that he could not hope to convince him if the Archbishop could not do so. Some of Elwell's supporters emigrated to America.

355 James Boswell, p.25. *Byrom's Diary. Boswell for the Defence 1769-1774.*

Three enterprising Elwell brothers

From *The Iron Elwells*: three Elwell brothers, Edward (bapt. 1736), William (bapt. 1737) and young John bought one eighth of the manor of Madeley in Shropshire in 1755. The following year the brothers began negotiating a sale of the property to Abraham Darby. In 1778, Darby agreed to supply 200 tons of pig-iron worth £6,700 annually to the brothers, who took responsibility for transport. William was appointed as a commissioner for the construction of the famous Iron Bridge over the Severn in 1775.

The Persehouses reappear in a place called Wasted Hayes or Walsted Hay, situated at the Delves near Wednesbury Forge. In the 17th century, it had belonged to John Persehouse of Reynolds Hall, Walsall. Richard Reynolds of Madeley, connected to the Darbys, entered into an agreement with a Birmingham ironmonger to take ironstone from Reynolds' land. Land between Wasted Hayes and Hickney Hayes featured in the will of wealthy William Elwell (1736-1793), who owned land and buildings in Park Street, Walsall as well as 'Wisemore' lands there. Elwells' pew in the old Walsall Church was as large as the Mayor's but William believed to "share and share alike" in relation to the fairness of his will. At one of three ironworks Edward Elwell owned machinery driven by a beam engine made by James Watt at his famous Soho foundry in Birmingham. This particular ironworks was at Hill Top, West Bromwich, where Edward produced cast iron tinned hollow ware. The beam engine was in constant use until 1904 when it was replaced. In the 1960s, the foundry became a factory of Associated Electrical Industries (AEI).[356]

Enclosures and the Enlightenment

Large tracts of land were allocated to the Dudley Estate by the Enclosure Act commissioners.[357] These were mostly in Netherton where the Parkes occupied a dwelling house on Gad's Lane, an area of Irish people. The land was quickly divided into fields and farmed. Writing in *The Land*, an occasional magazine about land rights, Fairlie remarked, "No kind of intervention on behalf of the landless poor should be allowed to disturb the invisible hand of economic

---

356 Charles J.L. Elwell, *The Iron Elwells,* pp.36-38, 43.

357 Parliament, *Enclosure Act.*

self-interest... more like an iron fist."[358] The last and most troublesome spate of English land enclosures were completed between circa 1750-1850. The Dudley agricultural community and farm hands must have felt the impacts of the enclosures as well as new scientific ideas that were coming along.

For the benefit of Jackson family readers: Reverend Joseph Jackson was a Proctor of Lichfield Cathedral, who did most of the work when *Linnaeus's Genera and Species Plantarum* was translated and published in 1783 by the Botanical Society of Lichfield.[359]

Electricity and the Enlightenment

Alessandro Volta managed to reorient the networks of European electricians by his discovery of the voltaic battery, announced from the small town of Como in Lombardy. Golinski points out that the traditional model, which has the Enlightenment in one place gradually spreading outwards, was inadequate.[360] Edward Bancroft (a Massachusetts-born chemist, electrician and spy) provides another example of how the ability of provincials to present themselves as original thinkers unsettled those who could not imagine the importance of new thinking contributing to knowledge.[361] When existing beliefs were challenged by open minds, enlightenment spread abroad. Resistant minds needed to accept that people and their beliefs could differ. During the 1800s, Elwell-Parker Ltd became rich from their application of electricity.

Canals and the Dudley Wards

Birmingham's first canal was opened in 1769, linking Birmingham to Wednesbury. There are many locks on canals local to this city, including the famous Guillotine Lock in Kings Norton, used to control the flow of water

---

358 Simon Fairlie, 'The final and most contentious wave of land enclosures in England occurred between 1750 and 1850' in *The Land* (n.d.) *http://www.thelandmagazine.org.uk* [accessed 13 April 2016].

359 Joseph Jackson, *Linnaeus's Genera and Species Plantarum,* for the Botanical Society of Lichfield (Lichfield, 1783).

360 Jan Golinski, 'Science in the Enlightenment, revisited', in *Hist. Sci.*, xlix (2011), p.223. Fn. 32 Lisbet Koerner, 'Carl Linnaeus in his time and place' in N. Jardine, J.A. Secord and E.C. Spary (eds). *Cultures of Natural History* (Cambridge, 1996), pp.145-162.

361 Jan Golinski, 'Science in the Enlightenment, revisited', in *Hist. Sci.*, xlix (2011), p.225.

between canals owned by different companies.[362] Gas Street basin was not always the terminus of the Birmingham Canal but began where the Alpha Tower now stands in Centenary Square. The Dudley Wards inherited the Dudley family descent of course from Humble Ward's time. William Lord Viscount Dudley was involved in the most expensive parliamentary Bills of 1791, which eventually gave assent to the Birmingham and Worcester Canal; G.W. Keeling was the consulting engineer.[363] For those interested in Birmingham Canal Statutes, the Earl of Dudley Estate Collections are accessible at Dudley Archives.[364]

---

362 Sarah Loat, *Birmingham – stuff you should know*, BBC Homepage (13 November 2014, last updated 2018). This page has been archived and is no longer updated. *http://www.bbc.co.uk/Birmingham/content/article/2008/04/15/Birmingham-facts-features.shtm* [accessed 26 February 2019].

363 Alan White, *Worcester and Birmingham Canal – Chronicles of the Cut* (Studley, Warwicks, 2005). G.W. Keeling was the consulting engineer to the SNB Co.

364 Dudley Archives, *The Earl of Dudley Estate Collections*, vol. 8 DE/6/12/.

Chapter 7

Wolverhampton Wonders?

THIS SAGA proceeds into the 19th century from Hanoverian to Victorian times with the Elwells along with a reappearance of the Tomlinsons in Sedgley. St. Thomas's and Elswall Pieces were clearly marked fields beside a route to Netherton on a sketch map based on Dudley's pre-enclosure plan of the 1780s.[365] The Elwells (alt. Elwall) were a Black Country family with strong links to Wolverhampton, Compton, Tettenhall and Penn; Daniel Elwell Tomlinson was a memorable relation (d. 1879). At this point the tree comprises just three generations up to 1899:

Great-great-Grandmother: Ann (Nancy b. Elwell)
m. 1. William Tomlinson, 2. John Hyde
|
Great-Grand-parents: Susannah (b. Hyde) married Edward Evans
|
Grandma: Annie (b. Evans)

Finishing this saga's history at 1899 is deliberate and intended to put the lives of these three generations into context of time/place, while slotting them into their ancestry as well as respecting the privacy of Grandma's living grandchildren, all born before 1946. Woodsetton, Sedgley, was where our

---

365 Edward Chitham, *The Story of Dudley* (Stroud, 2014), illus. Figure 45, p.110, 'Parts of Church Field and Peacocks Field based on the pre-enclosure plan'.

ancestor Daniel Elwell senior (b.1754) lived with his wife Esther (b. Turley, baptised Christmas Day 1756). They married in 1776, it was their son Daniel Elwell junior (b.1781) a nailer who was father to Great-great-Grandmother Ann (Nancy) Elwell (1796-1872).

Less is known of the Hydes' and Evans' paternal lines.

In the mid-1700s, canals solved the industrial transport problems of moving raw materials inwards and finished goods outwards. Farmers benefited also as new methods came with an Agrarian Revolution; they needed the means of bringing manure and fertilisers inward and taking their produce outward.[366] Edward Evans was a labourer in 1858, the year he married Annie, later he became a canal worker. Eventually Grandma Evans and siblings grew up in Canal Bridge House, Compton, near Wolverhampton. This saga throughout the 1800s, around Wolverhampton and the Black Country, mostly involves two themes: the Elwell family and the 'Canal Age'.

The Elwell family

Gradual settlement along Cotwallend Lane and to its south was probably late or post-medieval, a John Elwell lived at Cotwall End House where he owned 70 acres.[367] Maybe at some time he was landlord to our family. He was probably John Elwell (1785-1859) who owned an estate at Cotwall End. Another Elwell, Arthur, was elected as surveyor of Cotwall End in the 1860s.

Intermarriages of leading families from 1802

There were several intermarriages: Edward Parkes and Sarah Elwell married in Sedgley on 27 September 1802, also a couple married in Dudley 1897 with parents' names: George and Sarah Parkes. The Spurriers had married into the Elwells when William Spurrier's daughter Carew married an Edward Elwell, a few years after 1811. He left the Army and practised as a surgeon on Walsall High Street until he returned to the iron industry. In 1811, a John Elwell married Ann Willetts. He moved to Sedgley and used the Staffordshire and Worcestershire Canal for carrying nails, chains, lamp brackets, cart fittings, vices and more. Goods were loaded aboard boats at Wombourne where John

---

366 *A Short History of Tettenhall, 8 The Canal and the Turnpike.*, illus. https://*www.historywebsite.co.uk/articles/Tettenhall/tetten08.htm* [accessed 26 October 2020].

367 Charles J.L. Elwell, *The Iron Elwells; A family Social History*, 2nd ed., rev. and enlarged (Ilfracombe, Devon, 1992), illus.

kept a warehouse. Correspondence was simply addressed to him by his name, Sedgley, near Wolverhampton. He lived at Sedgley Manor House. Spurriers were ironmongers although the meaning then would be iron industrialists. Carew's niece married Edward's nephew, Paul of Evelith Manor, whose elder brother Charles John Elwell resided at Compton Hall circa 1868.[368]

Eventually Edward Elwell acquired Wednesbury Forge and installed steam engines where there had been water power previously. Messrs Holden and Willetts had served the munitions needs of the Napoleonic Wars (1803-1815) during their time there. The Napoleonic Wars had boosted canal usage but canals declined as military traffic dwindled.[369] Depleted canal trade struggled on for many years then faced competition to rail against, yes trains were arriving.

Georgiana's diary mentioned a long talk with Miss Ward, more evidence that the Elwells and Dudley Wards mixed.[370] Indeed, Georgiana was married to Revd. Peter Potter by her vicar brother Henry at St. James' in October 1860. The other couple were another brother, Alfred Elwell, and Susan Ward, the Twiggs' governess. *The Wednesbury and West Bromwich Advertiser* reported that there were many flags and festoons on the occasion of Georgiana's wedding. Regrettably a cannon was accidentally discharged and Mr Malpass was injured. Georgiana's wedding settlement was £6,000.

A Wednesbury Forge couple, Edward Elwell married 'Harriette Ward' (b.1845) at St. Mary's, Shrewsbury, on 18 May 1871. The bride was a younger daughter of the late W.R. Ward, Esquire, Royal Naval Commander and she was said to have died on the day of her Grandson's wedding circa May 1916, in Llanllwchaiarn, Montgomeryshire. Their wedding was reported in *The Belfast Newsletter*, the vicar being Edward Elwell Esquire of Wednesbury.[371] This matches another source: Edward and Carew's eldest son Edward married 'Harriet' Ward. Edward retired to Montgomeryshire and did what Elwells often did: became a churchwarden (and J.P., d.1926).[372] William Spurrier, a Walsall

---

368 *A Lady of Wednesbury Forge; The Diary of Georgiana Elwell of Wednesbury Forge 1868-1869*, ed. Charles J.L. Elwell. Cover design: C.J. Baker (Clebak), (A Black Country Society publication 1976, rev. and reprinted 2011), p.25. Fn. 4 Compton Hall, near Wolverhampton, residence of Charles John Elwell, an elder brother of Paul of Evelith.

369 John Watney, *The Industrial Revolution*, Pitkin, (n.d.), b.&w. and col. illus.

370 *A Lady of Wednesbury Forge.*

371 Marriage Notices, *The Belfast Newsletter* (Belfast, Northern Ireland, 26 May 1871), no. 55,030, Year CXXXIII.

372 Charles J.L. Elwell, *The Iron Elwells,* pp.58, 66-67, 70, 84-85.

factor, son of Walter Spurrier, twice Mayor of Walsall, married Maria. Their descendants through Jane was Paul Elwell of the famous Wolverhampton firm known as Elwell-Parker Ltd. The company registered patents for dynamos, magnetos and electrically driven vehicles. The Elwells and the Spurriers shared the same pew in Walsall Parish Church. Georgiana's family were friends with many clergy from local parishes in Wednesbury, Walsall, Wolverhampton and West Bromwich. Relatives visited their home, 'Wednesbury Forge House', travelling from Lichfield, Walsall, Wolverhampton, Dudley and Shifnal.[373] Indeed, William Elwell Walker was Mayor of Dudley 1885-1886. In the previous century, William Elwell (1736-1793) had held the same office.[374] Grandma's son was a Walsall councillor still remembered for his good works at an aunt's funeral in the late 20th century.

Back in 1818 Daniel Elwell was recorded as making snaffles in Dudley Square.[375] Nowadays it would be waffles! Snaffles were much needed 'bits' for equipping and controlling horses. Elwells had diverse expectations and occupations. The forge at Heath Mill in Wombourne was operated by the youngest son of the Mayor of Walsall, John Elwell. This John lived at Heath House, which in the same year, 1818, was described as a "genteel mansion" having previously belonged to the Foley 'iron empire' along the river Stour.

Ellowes Hall (alt. Ellers) and Cotwall End (alt. Cotwallend), Sedgley

Ellowes Hall was built and inhabited in 1821 by John Turton Fereday, who bought the estate from his uncle, ironmaster Samuel Fereday. 'Ellers' reflected the taste of S. Fereday, Esq.:

> "in ornamental gardening, several varieties of the most delicious and highly flavoured fruits are cultivated in great profusion."[376]

---

373 *A Lady of Wednesbury Forge.*

374 Charles J.L. Elwell, *Black Country Essays and Reviews*, The Black Country Society (Kingswinford, 1998), b.&w. illus. Image of William Elwell (1736-1793) from a miniature from the possession of William Edward Elwell of Ripon, p.161 also a group picture containing Charles E. Elwell and Edward Elwell III, p.116.

375 Parsons and Bradshaw, *Staffordshire*, vol. 3, p.114 of 262.

376 *Lower Gornal, The Ellowes*, C.D. Morris, All Rights Reserved (updated 2020). Ellers, on the west side of this parish (Sedgley), is a pleasing specimen of the taste of S. Fereday, Esq. in *Parson & Bradshaw's Staffordshire General & Commercial Direct*ory. *http://www.lowergornal.co.uk/* [first accessed 12 February 2017, again 15 October 2020].

The Feredays had been a Sedgley family of the Gornals since the 1600s at least. One of Samuel's sons, whose Christian name was Dudley, endowed St. John's College, Oxford, with £20,000 (in 1998 that would be worth upwards of £600,000). The subsequent owner of Ellowes Hall had a saga history surname, John Latty Bickley, another coal and ironmaster. Further ironmasters were to live there until it became home to a daughter of the Dudley Wards when she married into Horace St. Pauls' family (owners of the Hall since 1872). Dunphy questioned whether Ellowes Hall took its name from a medieval owner called Ellow (synonymous in the 16th and 17th centuries with Elwall) or did that family take their name from the estate?[377] The West Lodge of Ellowes Hall provided an entrance from Cotwall End Road, Sedgley. There was a time when residents of Cotwall End (alt. Cotwallend) fetched their water from Gornal Wood, a basic reminder of life's hardships.[378]

In 1772, two acres, a rood and 12 perches of land were charitably gifted in Hayley Field, Cotwall End, by Ann Webb for 30 poor housekeepers (30 shillings each). Cotwall End District was composed of three settlements in 1847:

> Cotwallend with 30 holdings;
> Sandfields with one settlement;
> Moden Hill with two settlements but not in Cotwallend.[379]

Great-great-Grandmother Ann (Nancy) Elwell

It is known from census data that Cotwall End was home to Great-great-Grandma Ann (b. Elwell, 1796-1872). 'Nancy' could have been given affectionately to her in later life as was customary to denote grandmothers (nans). She married William Tomlinson in Sedgley; he was a very young father but surely people were still aware of the arranged marriages of gentry youth, which had been normal for centuries? Perhaps not. Unfortunately, this saga knows little

---

377 Dudley Teacher's Centre, Angus Dunphy, 'The Ellowes, Its Owners and Times' in Charles J.L. Elwell, *Black Country Essays and Reviews*, The Black Country Society (Kingswinford, 1998), pp.159-160.

378 *Lower Gornal, The Ellowes*, C.D. Morris, All Rights Reserved (updated 2020).

379 Dudley Metropolitan Borough Council, 'Township of Sedgley 1750', produced by John Hemingway and Jennifer Foster (Dudley, 2006), bibliog. col. map, pdfs. *https://www.dudley.gov.uk/residents/planning/historic-environment/historic-maps-of-dudley/* [accessed 16 October 2020]. (Dudley's historic maps can be viewed from 1307 to the present day). 'Cotwallend Township'.

about William, except that he was son or nephew to local Barnard Tomlinson whose brother Cornelius was christened in 1784 at Straits, Cotwallend.

William's name was on a Burial Index dated 4 May 1823. His children with Ann by 1841 were Daniel (who throughout his life went by 'Elwell Tomlinson', b.1818), Thomas (b.1821), and Ruth (b.1823). Ann's second husband was John Hyde of Wombourne (1801-1849) a nailer, they married at St. Peter's, Wolverhampton, in 1826. John was age 40 in 1841, it's doubtful he made 50. Ann's status became Mrs Hyde, born Elwell (late Tomlinson), which is evident from birth and census information. The Hyde children, all born in Sedgley, were: John (1833), William (1835), Great-Grandmother Susannah (1837) and Benjamin (1840). A Ruth Hyde witnessed a boatman's wedding between Emma and Thomas Dyson at St. Peter's on 3 May 1856.[380]

Instances of Jacksons and Elwells of Cotwall End

There were instances of Jacksons in Cotwall End, Sedgley, the place where Ann Nancy lived. Three generations of Barnard Tomlinsons resided nearby. A Jackson child enters the story here in relation to Esther Elwell (b. Turley) later Roberts. She had a daughter Susannah Roberts (b.1789), whose son was called William Jackson. Ann had four half siblings, including this William Jackson. Little is sure except the boy's father's name was probably William Jackson also. A William Jackson appeared in the 1860 *Post Office Directory of Staffordshire* as an Upper Gornal tailor.[381] At Hinksford Lock too, there was a William Jackson connected with the Old Bush Inn (year unknown).

A 21st century Jackson step-family and their connection to Dudley arose along the trajectory of this saga [Peter Jackson died on 4 April 2020]. They were descendants of Edward Baron Sutton Dudley 25th and his wife Theodosia (born Harington), an amazing coincidence! It means a Dudley union containing the name Jackson came to notice halfway along this saga tree, living in Cotwallend as step-relations to the Elwell family. When Angela Jackson revealed her forebears were Dudley people it was worth investigating further. These Jacksons turned out to be a current step-family descending from the legitimate Wards' line whereas this saga's descent was from Baron Sutton

---

380 *Holt's database of Wolverhampton boats, boaters and their families*, collated by Norman Holt from parish registers, pdf.

381 *Post Office Directory of Staffordshire*, ed. by E.R. Kelly (London, 1860), with map engraved expressly for the work and corrected to the time of publication.

Dudley 25th's line with Elizabeth Tomlinson. Realising the connection resulted in much mirth and mock curtseying when we discovered we were so related. The significant marriage evidence was dated 1933, at Mutford, between Gertrude Harriet Ward and Frank Alfred Jackson: her parents were William Ambrose Ward and his wife Gertrude Rosamund (b. Hayes, 1889-1961).

At Dudley Archives a set of transcripts can be found, the work of Dudley Public Library.[382] Some Jacson burials were recorded:

> Thomas son to Larance Jacson 1540?;
> Marian daughter to Larance Jacson 1553;
> Margeri Jacson, wido-bureed 1553.

Angela Jackson with her first grandchild, born around midnight New Year 2020/21 during the Covid-19 lockdown.

An Arthur Harrison (possibly related to the Wards) married Elizabeth Jacson. The first of the transcript series has a Jacson family, no date, but data included Elizabeth, Henry, Lawrence, Margery, Marian and Thomas.

William Ambrose Ward m. Gertrude Rosamund (b. Hayes, 1889-1961), Angela's Great-Grandparents.

Road route 1823, avoiding Tettenhall ridge

Tettenhall Road was under the control of the Wolverhampton Turnpike Trust of which Sir John Wrottesley was a trustee (Sedgley Beacon Tower was built in 1846 by Lord Wrottesley, an amateur astronomer). How did Compton Road and Tettenhall Road come to be improved? The old London to Holyhead Road left Wolverhampton by Tettenhall Road, crossing the Smestow Bridge about 20 yards east of the New Bridge. This was important because after the Act of Union with Ireland in 1801, 100 Irish MPs used the road

382 Dudley Public Libraries, *Dudley*, ed. by J.S. Roper (Transcript series).

to attend Parliament in London. Their political clout was enough to ensure improvement of this important road. Eventually Parliament brought Thomas Telford to the task but rejected his ideas. A new line of road out of Wolverhampton to Aldersley was built instead by the Turnpike Trust and was completed in 1823, avoiding Tettenhall ridge.[383] Telford grudgingly acknowledged the route's good points. Nevertheless, the new road isolated Tettenhall village and church from Upper Green, which was considered generally to be a pity. No doubt local saga relatives had plenty to say about the matter.

Sedgley

Dudley's holdings on Priory Lane, Sedgley, is where marker stones remain to be seen in boundary walls.[384] Hemingway used the word 'palimpsest' to represent Sedgley's capability to preserve its sense of history along with its survival as a live community. A 'palimpsest' was the Greek word for a manuscript on which one history after another was written, erased and re-written. Sedgley deserves fame for its unique early industrial activity which heralded the Industrial Revolution of the 19th century. The Bull Ring, was a small market area where baiting with purpose bred Staffordshire bull terriers took place. A sketch map boundary distance was given as over 17 miles and the highest point, Sedgley Beacon, 777 feet above sea level.[385] All Saints, Sedgley, was rebuilt in 1826-1827, it commemorates a Reverend Elwell and an interior wall of the church has a plaque in memory of Mary Ann Elwell, who had died age 22 on 10 August, 1810.

Cholera 1832

Somehow Ann Nancy and John Hyde lived through the cholera epidemic that struck Sedgley in 1832. It was merciless and conditions were harsh for those who survived epidemics. Cholera morbus was commonly called Indian or Asiatic cholera. On 6 August, Rev. Girdlestone and other local clergy were amongst the gentlemen on a newly formed Board of Health sanctioned by

383 *A Short History of Tettenhall, 8.* Act of Union with Ireland 1801.

384 Dudley Metropolitan Borough Council, 'Township of Sedgley 1750', John Hemingway and Jennifer Foster. *https://www.dudley.gov.uk/residents/planning/historic-environment/historic-maps-of-dudley/* [accessed 16 October 2020]. (Dudley's historic maps can be viewed from 1307 to the present day). 'Sedgley Township'.

385 Ron Baker (died 1918), Map of the Nine Villages making up the Ancient Manor of Sedgley. Based on the 1844 Tithe Survey. Sketch map by Tom Bennett, refined by Ron Baker (1996). *http://www.sedgleylocalhistory.org.uk/Map.html* [accessed 14 October 2020].

the Privy Council. W. Marsh was an overseer on the Board aided by J. Elwell, J.P. Roberts, W. Darby and others.[386] Chitham wrote that churchwarden Joseph Bennitt was so horrified by the cholera outbreak that he signed a poster dated 22 September 1832 to say Wednesday 26 September would be "a day of humiliation."[387] Along with others, Cornelius Cartwright gave £10 for those "brought to a state of destitution" by the aftermath of cholera in Dudley. In 1843 the number of burials recorded included 7-week-old baby George Henry Bennett from Bumble Hole. Few of those buried had Old Testament names, as Nonconformist names were becoming popular, although the Daniel Tomlinsons were exceptions.[388] The cholera deaths must have been devastating while anyone of Catholic religion also still faced lingering objections from Protestants and Nonconformists. Life must have been very hard.

The Earl of Dudley Estate Collection, 1836

Dudley Archives holds *The Earl of Dudley Estate Collections*, which includes Black Country canal history, Tettenhall was mentioned in 1836.[389] This is relevant to the lives of Great-Grandparents Susannah (b. Hyde) and Edward Evans when they resided in a busy Canal House serving the Staffordshire and Worcestershire Canal. Edward was born in Chester in 1836 and was a year older than Susannah. He came from Steam Mill Street and could have journeyed to the Compton or Wolverhampton area and beyond via the Shropshire Union Canal, which operated from the north west coast, Ellesmere Port and Chester and joining the Staffordshire & Worcestershire

---

386 *Cholera outbreak in Sedgley in 1832*. Report from Sedgley Parish Register on the cholera outbreak in Sedgley in 1832. Transcribed by Christine Elllis. *http://www.sedgleymanor.com/historical/cholera1832html* [accessed 12 February 2017].

387 Edward Chitham, *The Story of Dudley*, pp.438-439.

388 Charles J.L. Elwell, *The Iron Elwells*, pp.21-22. (Christian names within the area included the name Daniel. There were few other Old Testament names, ten Anns, only one Hanna, no mention of Esther.)

389 Dudley Archives, *The Earl of Dudley Estate Collections*, Canals, vol. 8, DE/6/12. Birmingham Canal: Acts of Parliament 1716-1818. [25 Geo III] 'An Act for Extending the Dudley Canal to the Birmingham Canal at or near Tipton Green, in the County of Stafford' (1785), DE/6/12/1/3. Birmingham Canal Navigation Act 1784. Tettenhall (1826), DE/6/12/22. Plan of the Birmingham Canal Navigations (1835), DE/6/12/3/24. Map of Basin and Wharves near Green's Forge, belonging to the Trustees of the late Earl of Dudley (Wombourne) (December 1838), DE/6/12/3/28. Plan of Railways, Canals and Roads between the Black Country and Birmingham (1841), DE/6/12/3/44.

Canal at Autherley Junction. *The Estate Collections* also referenced a map of wharves and basin near Green's Forge, Wombourne.

Railway plan of 1841

A plan of 1841 was devoted to railways, canals and roads between the Black Country and Birmingham. Railways were coming, bringing serious economic competition and they would eventually displace canals.

Tithe Survey, 1844

Ron Baker's refinement to Tom Bennett's sketch map of Sedgley clearly shows and names the nine villages of Sedgley Manor based on an 1844 Tithe Survey: comprising, Sedgley, Gospel End, Cotwall End, Upper Gornal, Lower Gornal, Woodsetton, Coseley, Ettingshall and Brierley.[390] Ron Baker's views of the manor are subject to copyright. By invitation his delightful artwork of old Sedgley can be viewed online via Sedgley Local History Society. Himley was outside the sketch map boundary to the south west and Dudley lay south of the sketch map across the village boundary. Brierley does not seem to feature so much in this saga as the other Sedgley villages, although the great majority of Elwells, whose social status have not been recorded, lived in parishes adjacent to Sedgley: mainly in Wolverhampton, Bilston, Tipton and Codsall but mostly Ettingshall, Woodsetton, Coseley, the Gornals, Gospel End and Cotwall End.

Crystal Palace, 1851

Cowley & James of Walsall, manufacturers of brass beds and brass chandeliers, which were accessible and affordable for the masses, exhibited at Crystal Palace. Encouraged by Prince Albert, they were prize-winners, partly for the simplicity of their bedstead design.[391] Elwell industrialists seem not to have exhibited at the Great Exhibition in 1851 because Wolverhampton politicians were preoccupied with railways and South Staffordshire minefields. The Council failed to reply to an invitation from the Royal Commission at this time of early business marketing methods. Elwell manufacturers were not located in central Wolverhampton and councillors were perhaps being awkward. However, it is certain the Elwells did go, from a letter written

390 Ron Baker, Map of the Nine Villages making up the Ancient Manor of Sedgley.

391 Centre for West Midlands History, Black Country History Day held at University of Birmingham (October, 2016).

by Carew Elwell (1790-1871) to her granddaughters at Wednesbury Forge dated 13 May 1860, Woods Hotel, (Furnival's Inn, Holborn):[392]

> "not too tired except for the dreadful shaking of the carriage... We shall soon be on our way to Sloane St. and Crystal Palace. Signed Grandmama."
>
> [Carew Elwell (1790-1871)]

The Evans Family

Susannah married Edward Evans on Valentine's Day 1858 in St. Thomas's, Dudley; both signed with the mark of a cross. Apart from various certificates, snippets of information about Susannah and Edward's children came from 20th century descendants. An elderly aunt tended to know much more about end of lives than beginnings and liked to talk about funerals and wills in dark, almost Victorian, style. The result is a bizarre array of accounts straight from human memory. Several of the sons-in-law were actually called Will, which adds comedy to tragedy.

Hannah of Tettenhall's husband Will died on Boxing Day, she was born in 1859 and lived to age 70. Harriet Jane (b.1860, Blacklay, Wombourne) became a domestic servant on Bridgnorth Road where the Evans' address was then Canal Bridge, Compton (B4161 road). A toll was collected mid-road at Tettenhall Old Bridge, the original route constructed across the canal in 1771 locally Listed. It was only a few yards south from the first New Bridge of 1823 when improvements were made to the London to Holyhead Road (A41).[393] It is likely that Edward's work took him there as older family members mentioned New Bridge. This 1823 bridge was replaced in the 1960s and a suburb east of the canal took the name 'Newbridge'. Henwood Road runs parallel to the canal and crops up in saga census records. Parker provides superb images of the Old Bridge, a passenger boat and many Tettenhall historic photographs and postcards.[394] The area was picturesque and the surroundings very pleasant. Edward died in the 1880s and Harriet eventually

---

392 *A Lady of Wednesbury Forge*, p.7.

393 The Society for All British and Irish Road Enthusiasts (SABRE), 'Tettenhall New Bridge' in *Reader's Digest*.

394 Bev Parker, *Tettenhall in Old Photographs*, courtesy of David Clare's collection of postcards. *https://www.historywebsite.co.uk* [accessed 11 November 2020]. Geoffrey Hancock, *A Tettenhall History: Images of England, Bilston, Tettenhall and Wednesfield. Broadside* (Tettenhall, n.d.). Mary Mills and Tracey Williams (Tempus Publishing, 1998).

married one of the lodgers taken in by Susannah after 1891, almost needless to say – his name was Will.

Saga surnames around Sedgley and Wolverhampton in 1860:[395]

Charles John Elwell	The Hall, Compton
Dews, Thomas	Shopkeeper, High Street
Edward Elwell	Spade and shovel maker of Lower Gornal
Elwell & Willets	Nail & chain manufacturers, High Street
Elwell, Henry B.	Postmaster, Queen Street, Wolverhampton
Elwell, Thomas & Sons	Merchants & Factors, 85 Union Street, Horseley Fields, Wolverhampton
Elwell Edward Barber esq.	Compton Road, Wolverhampton
Hyde, Benjamin	Farmer, Wolverhampton Road
Wilkes, Abel	Tailor at Gornal

Farmer Benjamin Hyde (1840-1901) could well have been John and Ann Nancy Hyde's son. He would have been 20 in 1860. Thomas Elwell bought Compton House, later Compton Hall, near Tettenhall. He was a London merchant and enthusiastic horticulturist who stocked his garden with grapes, nectarines, peaches and figs. It is said elsewhere that the family home of Thomas Parker of Elwell-Parker Ltd eventually became The Manor House, Upper Green, Tettenhall. He had lived previously on St. Jude's Road, Tettenhall.[396]

Next Evans children

Great-Aunt Mary was born in 1861, her husband, whose name was not Will, though his surname was Hill, worked at Chillington Tool Works, Tettenhall. Her brother Great-Uncle Will (b. circa. 1863) was age 18 in 1881. Mary was the one who cared for her elderly mother. The address: Roseberry Terrace, Henwood Road, Tettenhall, was relevant in some unknown way. In later life Susannah was a widow of independent means. She died at the end of WWI, her funeral was at Compton and she was buried at Tettenhall.

---

395 *Post Office Directory of Staffordshire* (1860).

396 *Thomas Parker; Elwell-Parker Limited,* illus., including, courtesy of Gail Tudor, an image of Thomas Parker's early cars outside his family home, The Manor House Upper Green Tettenhall. *http://www.localhistory.scit.wlv.ac.uk/genealogy/Parker.ElwellParker.htm* [accessed 10 October 2009]. *Crocker's Directory*, 'Entry for Paul Bedford Elwell' (1883).

A couple named Edward and Hannah Evans worked Wolverhampton canal boats around 1858-1860. They had a son William and a daughter Mary (no Ann) but neither of these infants' baptism dates in the *Holt Index* matched saga births. One of Great-Aunt Mary's brothers fell in love with a Colonel's daughter when he was in India with the Army. He returned to Britain; such unsuitable feelings were regarded as utterly scandalous. In time it may not have been the end of the story because it seems a Colonel returned to the Tettenhall area too. J.L. Elwell wrote of a Frederick Joseph Charles Elwall, Indian Army Colonel.[397]

Mary Evans, born 1861, photograph courtesy of Dennis family.

Jane came after Will, age 15 in 1881, her husband was Will Powell, a file-maker by trade and a postman in 1901. Perhaps he was acquainted with Wolverhampton Postmaster Henry B. Elwell? Will was hardworking, he had a smallholding on Henwood Lane as well as making locks in his garden shed.

Excerpts from A Lady of Wednesbury Forge, 1867-1868

Rev. Henry Elwell wrote in a letter to his sister Georgy dated 24 October 1867, Wednesbury:[398]

> "The servants are kicking up a row in their bedroom over my head, walking about etc… Fred has just commenced playing down below…"

It was the writing of an educated man, interspersed with vulgar asides, such as "pills as big as horse balls…" and "the silent sow sucks all the broth."

397 Charles J.L. Elwell, *The Iron Elwells*, p.28.

398 *A Lady of Wednesbury Forge*, pp.8-9, 10-12, 42. Fn. 3 W.C.B.E.'s sister Emily Mary, who later married the Rev. Arthur Law. He succeeded his father-in-law as Rector of Dauntsey, Wiltshire Fn. 8 W.C.B. Elwell.

Siblings Pattie, Althea (Allie) and Darwell (Dar) Dudley were friends of the Elwells. Another Dudley/Elwell wedding was to take place as Althea was to marry Henry Elwell. She penned to Georgiana Elwell (Georgie) on 7 January, 1868:

> "we shall have a quiet wedding I think."

Henry wrote from 6 Broad Street, Oxford, to his sister Georgy, on 11 March 1868:

> "Allie… and Pattie came down to Birmingham for the day. We went into a good many shops and bought many varieties of merchandise. I went in for about £120 of furniture at Chamberlain and King's. Next Sunday I am to preach a service in a place called Waterloo… I suppose you can talk French like a native now. It may afford you some consolation to think that you will probably forget most of it in a very short time after leaving France… as you were so unwell last time. Dover and Calais is the shortest way of any."

Penn is mentioned in *Iron Elwells*. Sophia Lakin was the daughter of a hatter of Penn and wife of Edward Elwell, who had acquired Wednesbury Forge early in the 1800s. They married in 1858 when he was 41 years old. His fortune was divided between his two brothers and his sister (after he had provided generously for his wife, they had no children). Could this wealth have anything to do with Great-Grandmother Susannah Hyde's gold sovereign left on the lockside tea-table on Sundays by her half-brother Daniel Elwell Tomlinson on behalf of someone unknown? At least one Great-great-aunt (of Susannah's siblings) experienced the same good fortune. Were these payments deliveries of inheritance monies arranged via a solicitor? Seeking Edward Elwell's sister's name on the charts in *Iron Elwells* is of little help, the author apologised for concentrating too much on the male lines and too little on the ladies. Great-Grandma Susannah seems to have been related to a wealthy Elwell line connected with Penn, based on the impression gained from Grandma's older siblings' memories of childhood visits to Susannah's mother Ann in "a big house." The children had to wear Sunday best and be perfectly behaved, seen but not heard.

A letter of 11 March 1868 was full of news of Henry's ordination and plans for moving from Oxford to Blackburn. William (Willie) C.B. Elwell was evidently a barrister awaiting briefs early in his career; Daniel Elwell Tomlinson would have been his contemporary. Sunday 13 September, 1868, brought a very good church collection: Henry preached and £30 odd was collected.

On Friday, 9 April, 1869, Georgiana's diary records:[399]

> "We went to Wolverhampton, had an interview with Cousin Paul."

Paul Elwell had offices in Queen Street. When Daniel delivered inheritance monies to Susannah and her sibling(s), did he obtain the sovereigns through a legal arrangement from an Elwell via a solicitor or bank?

Ann (Nancy) Hyde was a widow age 75 and living in St. Benedict's Parish with her son Daniel Elwell Tomlinson, a coal miner when he was age 52. Other Elwells lived only two doors away. Daniel died in 1879, he seems to have been a kind, caring person. His mother Ann died in Blacklay, Wombourne in 1872. Grandma might have remembered Daniel from when she was up to eight years old, which suggests that her older siblings went to his mother's home in earlier times or they visited a different household, a wealthy Elwell home perhaps. Where the sovereigns came from remains a family mystery but whatever the explanation Susannah's coin was delivered in person to her at the lockside by Daniel.

There were Elwell cousins in Montreal. One of them, Emily, visited England to see her Uncle Arthur of Penn. Paul Evelith's son Charles proposed to her in Sedgley, they married and lived at Penn for a time. When she died in 1899, Charles and his only daughter moved to the Laurels, Sedgley, the Uncle Arthur's old house. Charles planted an orchard, which he enjoyed until he died in 1924.[400]

Elwell-Parker Limited

During the 1800s, Wolverhampton Elwell-Parker Ltd became rich from their application of electricity. This company's history was packed full of accolades too extensive for here. Second son of Wolverhampton merchant Paul Elwell, Paul Bedford Elwell (b. 1853 in Albrighton) managed a works making nails and employed 100 hands. He was educated at King's College,

399 *A Lady of Wednesbury Forge*, pp.19, 34, 42-43. Fn. 7 Paul Elwell had offices in Queen's Street, p.36. *Wednesbury and West Bromwich Advertiser* (October, 1869), pp.42-43.

400 Charles J.L. Elwell, *The Iron Elwells*, p.66.

London, where he obtained a distinction in mathematics. Then he spent a year in Liege, France, studying coal mining and iron manufacturing. Paul and his Wulfrunian wife (native of Wolverhampton) Elizabeth lived in Shifnal, Shropshire, according to the *1881 Census*. His first registered patent was for nail-making machinery in 1876. His third was for Venetian blinds.

Thomas Parker was linked to Coalbrookdale and was in close proximity to the Darbys. He moved to Wolverhampton from Coalbrookdale in October 1882 and joined the Patent Tip & Horse Shoe Company that Paul Bedford Elwell had founded. At first Elwell had little knowledge of electricity and left that side of the business to Thomas. Once they began building dynamos, an order was received from the Manchester Edison Company for which they received £1,000 in advance. Two name changes later, aided by incoming cash, the company became Elwell-Parker Limited. Their Commercial Road location was close to Chillington Wharf on the Birmingham Canal. Several of Elwell's relations had invested generously in the company. Elwell spoke of occasionally using his telephone cable for the dual purpose of carrying power for lighting whilst also receiving operatic music from the Wolverhampton Theatre ten miles away. In 1883, *Crocker's Directory* listed him as managing director of the Patent Economic Coal Company Limited. Evidently he had additional business interests other than solely to his partner, Thomas. Nevertheless, the company designed and constructed the electrical plant for driving the Blackpool Tramway. Work began on the motors and dynamos in 1884. In 1887 the first electric-powered submarine, *Nautilus*, was fitted with an Elwell-Parker E.P.S. battery. Of this tramway, wealthy goldminer from Australia James Oddie, said:

> "This line is one of the sweetest things in the Empire."

All this explanation leads to the fact that these Elwells were very well off. However, Paul Bedford Elwell left the company in 1887 due to a large debt from the failure of his Bush Hill Estate investments. Worse still, he lost his wife Elizabeth to typhoid. Later he was responsible for the electrification of the Sydney tramways in Australia and he died there on 10 September 1899, aged only 46.[401]

---

401 *Thomas Parker, Elwell-Parker, Limited,* illus., including, courtesy of Gail Tudor, an image of Thomas Parker's early cars outside his family home, The Manor House, Upper Green, Tettenhall. *Crocker's Directory*, 'Entry for Paul Bedford Elwell' (1883).

The Canal Age

Canal lock-keepers and boatmen, 1870s

Lock-keepers sometimes acted as toll collectors and boat gaugers but their main role was to see boatmen quickly through the lock. They protected the lock and ensured boatmen neither wasted water nor damaged lock gates. The Birmingham Canal Navigation Company concentrated the gauging of its boats and those of other firms at Smethwick and Tipton. The names of boat builders appear on gauging tables. Wilkes contains a chapter about accessing records, including of gauging tables. There is also a reference to Edward-Paget Tomlinson's *Colours of the Cut* about canal art and boat markings.[402] *Holt's database of Wolverhampton boats, boaters and their families* can be downloaded online.[403] Another useful database obtainable via The Museum Collection is *John Roberts Waterways Index*.[404]

Quoting Julian Holland:

> "Canal boats were gauged for tolls by measuring the height of the gunwale above the water line. This measurement corresponded to a list of charges depending upon the type of cargo being carried."[405]

Men with little education and literacy were very clever at mathematics when it came to loading boats precisely and were respected for their skills. However, boatmen also had the reputation of being heavy drinkers. They often stabled their horses overnight at canal inns and canal sides, such as at Susannah's for tuppence (presumably per horse). Boatmen and boatwomen sat apart in inns and between drinks the boatmen loved to sing and dance – other talents they possessed.

From *Our Canal Population*:

> "Big burly men are wonderfully light of foot and keep time accurately."[406]

---

402 Sue Wilkes, *Tracing Your Canal Ancestors*; a Guide for Family Historians (Barnsley, 2011), pp.38, 42-43, 78-81, 84, 94, 122-125, 127. Edward Paget-Tomlinson, *Colours of the Cut* (2004). (Landmark Countryside Collection).

403 *Holt's database of Wolverhampton boats, boaters and their families*, collated by Norman Holt from parish registers, pdf.

404 *John Roberts Waterways Index*, *www.canalmuseum.com* [not accessed].

405 Julian Holland, *Canal Recollections; A Pictorial Record* (London, 2002), p.56.

406 Sue Wilkes, *Tracing Your Canal Ancestors – Our Canal Population* (1879).

By the mid-1870s wages had not changed significantly. In the Birmingham area a man working a slow boat averaged 20-25 shillings per week after feeding and stabling a horse. The carrier Heath & Sons' captains received £9 to journey for a week between Stourport and Manchester. John Crowley, a partner in Wolverhampton-based carrier firm Crowley, Hickin, Batty & Co. is quoted:

> "Many of the boatmen are very trustworthy, honest, moral and sober but many of them are very much the reverse."

Giving out Bibles and prayer books to boatmen and those hit by cholera or mourning lost souls in 1832 was a way good people responded to the needy. An attempt by reformers failed to set up a hostel in Wolverhampton in the late 1880s for boat children under 14 to be 'boarded out' at special schools during term-time then allowed back to their boats during school holidays. Parents did not want it. These are the people the saga's Evans family would have mixed with every working day. Boat people and navvies, who dug the canals, used nicknames as this saga's family did. Fellows, Morton & Clayton were one of the largest canal carriers in Britain, being the merger of three separate Birmingham companies, their boatmen were nicknamed 'Joshers' after the name of Joshua Fellows. From the 1870s until 1920, FMC operated steam narrow boats.[407]

Ann Evans, born 1871, photograph courtesy of Dennis family.

Grandma Annie Evans (1871-1928)

Great-great-Grandmother Ann Nancy Hyde (b. Elwell) died in 1872, the year after Grandma Annie Evans was born. According to family members, Grandma treasured nostalgic memories of her childhood and young years beside the Staffordshire and Worcestershire Canal. She reminisced about places near Wolverhampton: mostly Tettenhall, Penn, Wombourne and Compton.

---

407 Julian Holland, *Canal Recollections*, p.60.

Birmingham to Wolverhampton Canal development, 1875

For transporting goods in their day, canals were a major improvement on packhorse tracks and poor roads, which had become inadequate as industry had advanced. The first canal near Dudley in 1775 went from Birmingham to Wolverhampton, by-passing Dudley town. When Dudley tunnel was constructed (from 1784) its route passed via former priory lands and under the Wolverhampton Road. A branch was cut to Wren's Nest, its staircase entrance being completed in 1840.[408] A late and more modern development on the canal system was Netherton tunnel in 1855. There were towpaths on both sides with gaslight (subsequently replaced by electric lighting). Canal companies competed for access to water, vital for sufficient depth for boats and for filling and emptying locks. A longstanding problem of Dudley's water supply was remedied by a new reservoir on Sedgley's border.

Staffordshire and Worcestershire Canal, initially called Wolverhampton Canal

The canal runs from Stourport at the northern end of the Severn Waterway continuing north to meet the Trent and Mersey Canal at Great Haywood near Stafford.[409] The Act of Parliament approving construction was passed on 14 May 1766, the same year work commenced on the Trent and Mersey Canal according to engineer James Brindley's 'Grand Cross' scheme, aimed to connect Hull, Liverpool and Bristol docks and to link the four main river estuaries of England's Mersey, Trent, Severn and Thames. It linked the Severn at Stourport to the Mersey at Great Haywood near Stafford, the Wolverhampton Canal opened to traffic in 1772. The canal was designed by Brindley who was assisted by Samuel Simcock and Thomas Dadford the elder. Brindley was both surveyor and chief engineer.

---

408 Edward Chitham, *The Story of Dudley*, pp.105-107, 173. Fn. 12 Hadfield, C. *Canals of the West Midlands* (New York, 1966), p.260.

409 Grace's Guide Ltd., *British Historical History. Staffordshire and Worcestershire Canal* (11 December 2016). *https://www.gracesguide.co.uk/staffordshire_and_worcestershire_canal* [accessed 26 October 2020].

Table 3 – Route of the Staffordshire & Worcs Canal (courtesy of Graces Guide Ltd.)	
From Stourton-on-Severn, Upper Basin, York Lock	The world's 1st inland port. The first part from Stourport to Compton was opened in 1770.
Falling Sands Lock no. 4	Scenery changes at southern. Kinver Edge, a cliff of red rock. Split iron bridge over this old lock. Viaduct carries Severn Valley Railway at Falling Sands.
Caldwell Lock lock no. 5	Another split iron bridge goes over this old lock.
Kidderminster Lock	St. Mary's Church.
	Cookley village, local sandstone tunnel beyond.
Stourton	Stourton & Dudley Canal join from west.
Kinver Lock	Kinver Edge offers views to the Cotswolds and Malvern Hills. Kinver was the home of Lady Jane Grey. Richard Foley was an influential entrepreneur, who owned furnaces, forges and slitting mills. His mill on the Stour at Kinver was the first one to aid nail rod production.
	Tunnels to Whittington. Whittington Hall reputedly has priest holes.
Hyde Lock	Exceptionally pretty.
	Dunsley Tunnel.
Stewpony Lock	Unusual octagonal toll cottage.
	Prestwood, Devil's Den. Gothersley Bridge.
Greensforge Lock near Ashwood	Circular Weir. Navigation Inn built 1767.
Hinksford Lock	Bends to Swindon where James Brindley's plan followed the contours of the land. Inns: The Green Man and Old Bush, linked to a William Jackson.
This is where the canal approaches Wombourne.	

Having grown up in this area, Annie often spoke of Wombourne as though she knew it well. Whether her grandfather John Hyde had any connection to Hyde Lock or whether her father Edward Evans helped out at the Bratch is lost in time. Bratch Locks on Bratch Lane, Wolverhampton, was absorbed into Wombourne in the 20th century. It is a very interesting place on the canal, comprising a staircase of locks, described on CanalScene.com as:

"one of the sweet points and hidden gems of the canal network."

Built by James Brindley and opened in 1772, later it was re-engineered as three separate locks with six gates, including unusual double gates between the locks. Two bridges are there plus a toll house and lock-keeper's cottage, the Georgian architecture unspoiled. Nearby there is a Victorian Pumping Station of 1895, which functioned to force lock water back to the top.

Table 4 – Continuing along the Staffordshire & Worcestershire Canal	
Botterham Lock	Flight of 2 locks in a staircase, Giggety Bridge.
The Bratch, Wombourne	Octagonal toll office, set of 3 locks raises the water level 30 feet in short length. Resident lock-keeper. Sedgley, Gospel End and Woodsetton are east of here.
Awbridge Lock	Approaching Wolverhampton west.
Whitwick	Mill Lock Bridge (no. 58).
Compton	Compton Bridge (no. 59) A454 Bridgnorth Road. Compton Lock Bridge (no. 60). Tettenhall Old Bridge (no. 61) Meadow View. Tettenhall New Bridge, A41 Tettenhall Road, Wolverhampton. The ongoing Staffs & Worcs Canal route north is lock free to Gailey near Stafford.
Aldersley Junction	Here the Birmingham Canal heads east, its original purpose being to deliver Black Country raw materials, minerals and coal, returning with sophisticated manufactured goods. Meanwhile the S&W skirted Wolverhampton west.
Autherley Junction	Half a mile from Aldersley, the Shropshire Union Canal joins the S&W, having come from the north coast via Ellesmere Port and Chester.
Hatherton Jn., Gailey, Penkridge, Great Haywood.	The S&W continues north through Gailey and Penkridge to Great Haywood, where it meets the Trent and Mersey Canal that escorts the River Trent to join it at Shardlow. The S&W Canal offered delicate china from the Staffordshire Potteries better protection from breakages than possible overland. Greater quantities reached Gloucester and Bristol safely.

Compton Bridge, Tettenhall in 1771, drawn by Eileen Wale.

Old postcard of Compton Bridge, Tettenhall.

Old postcard of the Lock at Compton.

Another view of the Lock at Compton.

Great-Grandfather Evans was said by contemporaries to be a lock-keeper in charge of a flight of locks. Maybe he covered the Compton to Bratch section. The Bratch is acknowledged as a very special place.[410] One imagines it would be magical to a child like Annie. Edward Evans could have ridden a horse from one lock to another, walked the towpath or hitched a float on a boat. In deep winter perhaps he skated, curling was played whenever Pelsall Canal froze.[411] By road he could have crossed Lower Penn on foot. These are fanciful thoughts because there are more questions about the great-grandparents' day-to-day lives than answers.

Work commenced at Compton Lock in 1770 and had taken a year to complete. Being the nearest lock to Wolverhampton, a great deal of the town's trade began to pass through.[412] Compton Lock by weir and bridge is now a Grade II listed building out of Wolverhampton. This bridge is number 60, Tettenhall Old Bridge 61 and Wombourne 43.[413] The Canal House, or lock-keeper's cottage as described in this source and where Grandma grew up, has been demolished. The carriageway that originally gave access to the dwelling was rebuilt in 1986 by the British Waterways Board. The original construction company, remarkably, stayed independent right up until nationalisation in 1947 but inevitably it fell into neglect when coal traffic finished. Its busiest time was before 1815 but thankfully it was restored in modern times for leisure and pleasure purposes. Compton Lock is now considered to be one of James Brindley's first operational locks, the prototype became standard for the narrow canal locks of most Midland canals.

Decline of the Canals

Birmingham canals reached a peak towards the end of the 19th century with the change to railway transportation, The canals spanned 160 miles and were used by over 60 coal merchants and carried 8.5 million tons of

---

410 Geoff Caine, *Canal Photos of England's Waterways Heritage*, commenced June 2006. Design by SRS Solutions (2020). *https://www.CanalScene.com* [accessed 26 October 2020].

411 Walsall Local History Centre, '8. Two Walsall Sporting Clubs, Now Extinct', *Billy Meikle's Window on Walsall. Local History in and around Walsall Metropolitan Borough* by Stuart Williams (staff of Centre) (Walsall, 2010), pp.24-27. (A series of articles based on the writings of William 'Billy Meikle').

412 *A Short History of Tettenhall, 8.*

413 British Listed Buildings, *Compton Lock, By-weir and Bridge 60*, bibliog., map. *https://britishlistedbuildings.co.u/101411688-compton-lock-by-weir-and-bridge* [accessed 6 October 2020].

cargo annually.[414] When railcars came into use there were halts at Darby End and Baptist End.[415] Canals were still viable, still hauled by horses and occasionally by men again. Like Wolverhampton canals, Birmingham canals were true wonders industrially and still are for leisure, pleasure and helping the environment.

Younger Evans children

Ted was Grandma's next youngest sibling (1873-1938), age 9 in 1881, he had a humorous gravestone in Tettenhall Churchyard. The tombstones were moved but the vicar said that there were records of the whereabouts of those not moved to the perimeter of the churchyard. Ted was twice married and gave the impression of being good fun to know. The next child was Frances, age 2 in 1881. As a housemaid in service, she worked for Mr and Mrs D'Arcy and their two small children. Mr D'Arcy was a solicitor in Upper Penn. Incidentally the Evans solicitors in Walsall were saga relations. Frances had another job later in life, working at an inn in Himley. Edward, Prince of Wales, used to spend weekends at Himley Hall, entertaining friends, including Mrs Freda Dudley Ward (this was before he fell in love with Mrs Simpson and abdicated the throne). He treated customers to a drink while Frances served and observed. Her husband was Albert Fowler from Weston-Super-Mare, a landscape gardener for the Bishop family at Shipton Hall.

Ruth was aged 5 in 1881, her husband Jack Giles grew kidney beans and rode a bicycle. He hailed from the Hailes of Buckinghamshire. Ruth and Jack's daughter married into the Ravenscroft family, sadly their youngest daughter died in a fire. Finally Z for Zilla Evans, Zill rhymes with Will of course. Her full name might have been Priscilla, her dates are unknown. She married Martin McDonough and they lived at the Waterworks House at the top of Tettenhall Rock, which sounds as romantic as a mini Dudley Castle. They suffered the sad loss of their daughter, Minnie, killed by a bomb in London during WW2.

Grandma Annie was recorded as being a cook in the household of R.N. Smythe (retired) at Hilton, Worfield, near Bridgnorth, which means

414 Lewis Braithwaite, The Use of Urban Canals: with Special Reference to Birmingham and the Black Country (Birmingham, 1970). Fn. 10, Charles Hadfield, *The Canals of the West Midlands* (1986), maps.

415 Edward Chitham, *The Story of Dudley*, p.189.

she was in service there prior to living in and cooking for the occupants of Hammerwich Hall. During her days at Worfield, Annie was picked up by a pony and trap to be driven down Bridgnorth Road to the Smythe residence. Chitham mentioned the Smythe family of Wombourne.[416]

Young Thomas Shaw had:

> "Smythie towles (tools) in the 1500s while Baillies had bellows.
> Humfrey Jukes had 'Smythie belleyes with stydie and other tooles'."

It seems that Robert Smyth was a Wombourne man who witnessed Thomas Shaw's will. Also Taplin wrote that Henry Smyth and Job Dighton were trustees of Lady Dame Elizabeth Barnard's will.[417] Hammerwich Hall belonged to Mr and Mrs Stretton, landed gentry, who had two daughters. Tragically Mr Stretton was killed in a pony trap accident coming home from a railway station. How sorrowful this event must have been for young Annie.

Happier times were ahead: Annie met Grandfather Thomas Cox in Hammerwich Church where he was a choir boy, no doubt purity personified. They married in Wolverhampton, 1894, and had a family as readers will have guessed.

416 Edward Chitham, *The Story of Dudley*, p.51.

417 John Taplin, *Shakespeare's Granddaughter and the Bagleys of Dudley: An Investigation of their Relationship and that of Others to the Last Direct Descendant of William Shakespeare. https://www.blackcountrysociety.co.uk/articles/bagley.htm* [accessed 30 March 2016].

Concise Index of People